He Said, She Said

A Devotional Guide to Cultivating a Life of Passion

Eddie Jones & Cindy Sproles
Christian Devotions Ministries

Published by:
Christian Devotions Ministries
P.O. Box 6494
Kingsport, TN 37663
www.christiandevotion.us |
books@christiandevotion.us

Published in association with Lighthouse Publishing of the Carolinas.

ISBN-13: 978-0-9822065-5-3
ISBN-10: 0-9822065-5-0

He Said, She Said:
A Devotional Guide to Cultivating a Life of Passion
Copyright 2011 by Christian Devotions Ministries

Available in print from your local bookstore,
online, or from the publisher at:
www.christiandevotion.us |
www.christiandevotionsbooks.com
books@christiandevotion.us

All scripture quotations, unless otherwise indicated, are taken from the HOLY BIBLE, NEW INTERNATIONAL VERSION®. NIV®. Copyright 1973, 1978, 1984 by International Bible Society. Used by permission of Zondervan. All rights reserved.

He **$**aid, *She Said*

Table of Contents

He Said, *She Said*

Introduction

He Said

*And, in the end, the love you take, is equal to the
love you make.*

The Beatles

Love is a four-letter word and that word is "work."

Perhaps you thought love an emotion, a passion produced by the touching of skin or a provocative glance. Maybe you thought it a "thing" to be had, a transitory emotion fueled by fondness that swelled to meet your physical needs. But feelings are fickle; they grow tired and demand stimulation. Love is a thing to be held in your heart, you thought. A deep longing revealed through thoughtful words, shared songs and distant dreams – a yearning for completeness found in the arms of another. Like a wispy specter gliding across a crowded room, the object you perceived as love took form as a handsome prince or ravishing maiden; it captured your heart, pulling you close as it whispered: "I am love. Taste and enjoy."

With naive wonder you believed its words. Oh how you believed: for to doubt meant banishment to the land of the lonely where bitterness and rejection reigned. And yet, deep inside you feared the thing you thought love wasn't real, couldn't last and

6

would, in the end, betray you.

You were wise to worry, for today — last week, last argument — you awoke to find a stranger in your house: an alien in work clothes and smelling of spit-up, sweat and fried food. The thing you thought Love? Gone. No note. No explanation for its sudden disappearance. Only emptiness in your heart.

"I am lost and alone," you whisper to God. "I have fallen out of love."

"Oh? And will you fall out of love with me, too? Will you leave me when I become too demanding, fat, wrinkled, old, sick, or lazy?"

"You could never be like that."

"And yet I am a part of this thing you say is too hard, for when you said, "I do" — I did. Don't you remember? You asked me to join you at the altar. Would you toss out My Love because it demands too much?"

"Love is too hard."

"No. Love isn't hard enough. But for your sake I have made it easy."

"You call this easy?"

"I've only asked you to love two things: Me and the one bound to you. How can you say love is hard when I allowed you to choose your partner?"

"I was mistaken."

"You were enchanted."

7

"*It* was a mistake."

"I don't make mistakes. Come. Let's stop this squabbling. I'll show you how to love. Here, take hold of my hand. Yes, of course I'll wait. Love is patient. Love allows you to grow until what seems urgent is replaced with the important. Perhaps this devotional journal will help. Learn from those who wrestle with love. See how he says one thing: she another. Yes, yes, I know they are just words but words are powerful, are they not? Come, open this book and let us begin this journey.

"First, though, let us begin to love our friend and your partner. Watch. Did you see? Could you not hear the warmth in the words when our friend thanked us? Simple words, "I'm sorry." And yet full of kindness, for Love is kind. It seeks to help and lift up, not put down. It offers what's best.

"No, no, you keep the praise and hugs. I was only showing you how to make love. Besides, Love does not envy. I am content to let you enjoy the applause. Love celebrates *our* accomplishments. It rejoices with others.

"Here, now. You have gone too far. Put away that haughty attitude. You were too quick to believe that *you* were the source of our friend's joy. Now look at yourself. You are deformed. Quick, get rid of the ego. It whispers nothing but lies. Love does not boast; it is not proud. Love has no room for something as puny as self. If you must brag, brag on your partner.

"*You* want to lead? Really? But we have just begun the

journey. Very well. Only remember; Love is not self-seeking and ours is a long journey. What? Nonsense! No, I'm sure I didn't mean to make you angry. Love is not easily angered. Come, now. Stop feeling sorry for yourself. That will take you nowhere but down. Here, dry your eye and let's study the stories that lead to a life of passion. They will guide you in the way of love.

"What? When? No I don't remember. Love keeps no record of wrongs. Very well. If you want my forgiveness you have it. I only ask that you forgive others with the same measure of mercy. Why? Because all make mistakes. Haven't you? Well, you can try, can't you? Fine. We will forgive our friend together. There, now. Doesn't that feel better? All that weight removed. It's impossible to make love and carry a grudge. You were wise to get rid of it.

"Careful. Don't go too fast. You must be alert to the evil that lurks about, for Love doesn't delight in evil. Oh? Is that what you think? But this is where you are wrong. The thing you find so intoxicating and lovely is scandalous. Yes, yes, I know what you see. I made the original. But this thing you lust after is a fraud: a mere idol. It will rob you of true love. What you think to be harmless is wickedness in disguise. Turn away quickly, before the idol blinds you to *true* Love. If you must hate, hate what is evil.

"Yes I shielded your eyes; I pulled you away. Love always protects: even to the point of death. Of course you can rest upon me. Love trust. It leans on the arms of another. Ah, so you *do* remember how it was to love. How in those early days you titled toward each other, planting the seeds of love.

"But of course trusting is hard. It leaves you vulnerable, open to attack. Well, try for me, won't you? Think of how you felt all those years ago when you eagerly awaited our friend's arrival. I know you have lost hope, don't I know. But I am with you. And besides we have traveled so far already. Would you turn back now? Hope again. Love always hopes. Love always perseveres, even when the journey is difficult. Even when those we love hurt us. Love endures. Grow faith; have hope. Make love.

"Look! We have arrived at the end of our journey. Yes, I am looking back. I *do* see the crowd behind you. Where did they come from? Why you, of course. They are the ones you loved. You *made* love through your acts of caring, for Love is an act, not a feeling. The work *of* love produces the emotion. That is why I call it: Making Love. Now go. Study. Read. Work.

"Is this not the passionate life you long for?"

Eddie Jones

He Said, *She Said*

She Said

...And I will always love you.
I will always love you.

Dolly Parton

I stepped onto a long and dusty road. Raised with the abiding love found in the Southern Appalachian Mountains, I was blinded by the examples I followed, unaccustomed to dirt gathering on my shoes or rocks scuffing the toes. Ahead of me lay the trail of a fantasy: except I didn't know it was a fantasy. I saw it in the distance, longed for it. I sought after this thing thinking once I'd caught it, the rest would be simple.

Love, I thought, would be nothing less than perfect. That life, the love life, would be aprons, children and white picket fences. Yes, little girls still believe in those fantasies and I was no exception. My mother loved my father: my brother his wife. There was no divorce in our family. They were, by all due rights, a flawless illustration of impeccable and polished love. Surely I'd have nothing less.

But the road for me was different. The gullies and potholes were hard on my shiny patent leather shoes. The toes simply couldn't withstand being dragged through the dirt and before I knew it, they were almost ruined. What kind of road had I chosen? Where was the promise of love gifted by my parents to me? I'd missed the mark. The rose of love I'd dreamt of withered and died. It left me stranded on a road hidden in a wilderness of dark. I couldn't see. Lost, I went to my knees to feel my way along.

Love does that to us — brings us to our knees. When we are on our knees we do not rein above anyone: rather we are positioned as a servant.

We do not *find* love. That person we are called to love may be found, but love itself surrounds us. We work to earn love: and to make love. We may find pleasure in the arms of another but love...ah, love is a gift.

Though blinded by our fantastic feelings of wonder we embark on the journey, trusting the one who stands before us is true, (Mr.) right and noble. We search for a *sign*, a confirmation that the one before us is THE one. Once we've placed a ring on their finger, we lean back, cross our arms and wait for the reward of a perfect union.

I crawled my way along the dark road, pulling myself across the dry, parched ground, rocks scraped away at my flesh until my heart was ripped from my chest and tossed aside, left for the vultures. Love, at least this love, was nothing but; it was a hellish nightmare of loneliness.

So I returned to my first love, the love of my Father.

"But Lord," I cried. "I do love you. But do *You* love me?"

Silence. Nothing but pain and suffering. No joy, no peace. Only a hole where love used to live.

"Do you really love me?" God asked, at last.

"Oh yes, Lord. I love you. I have crawled through the darkness to love you."

"Then trust me. Love does not deceive. It does not harm. Love is work. Hard work. Like a lumberjack sawing the trunk of a massive tree, it takes a partner willing to pull when you push and even more so, willing to push when you pull."

God lifted me from the mire and placed me on a pedestal. He cleaned my shoes with His cloak, spit on His finger and soothed my wounds.

I can speak to the lie that love is easy for I have learned is it not. I can also speak to the truth that love is alive, that it nurtures and fulfills, for I have lived it.

Love is found in the relationship, the heart of the one you call as your mate. It is the tender touch of your spouse that shoots the thrill of passion through you. It is the early morning mist, the mid-day breeze, and the evening chill. Love is the promise of today and the hope of tomorrow, but love is nothing without God. To love Him first and as we love ourselves, and to love another in this same way...this is love.

As you read through the pages of this book I pray you will

see the many facets of love. I hope you will come to see the ring God has placed on *your* finger as an unbroken continuance of your love for the Father, your spouse, your family, and yourself.

I pray you will seek the passion that is made by loving *with all your heart, soul and mind.* The road is not easy. Your hands and knees may be bloodied, your heart broken, but stand firm because *his love endures forever.*

Love was not easy for Abraham when he was asked to sacrifice Isaac. It was not easy for Esther to stand before the king and plead for her people. Nor was it easy for Mary as she watched the sacrifice of her son...God's son. Love is given as a gift but we must work to make it a passion.

Knock and the door will be opened...seek and you will find the true passion of love when you love *as He first loved.* Cultivate a deeper relationship with Christ and He will enrich the passion of your relationship with Him and with the one you love.

Cindy Sproles

Romance, Rings & Ringtones In Bed

Loving Your Mate

Puppy Love

He Said

Place me like a seal over your heart, like a seal on your arm; for love is as strong as death, its jealousy unyielding as the grave. It burns like blazing fire, like a mighty flame.
Song of Solomon 8:6 NIV

I have a box of love notes I keep from my wife. The birthday cards and scraps of paper remind me of lips I kissed and tears I dried before I met my bride. I don't know if these relics of my broken heart are an act of unfaithfulness or simply a sad testimony to the passion a romantic who loved... and lost in the pursuit of puppy love.

First Kiss: We met in her basement for our first kiss. Everything I knew about smooching I'd learned from the movie *Love Story*. Ryan O'Neal and Ali McGraw kissed a lot: mostly with their eyes closed. This seemed only natural since the idea of standing that close to anyone, much less a pretty girl, terrified me. But there we were, two high school freshmen preparing to seal our love with lips coated in ketchup and mustard and hot dog chili. I advanced; she moved. I hit a cinder block wall. My aim improved but I never fully recovered from the miss... our first kiss that came moments later.

First Love: Like so many high school sweethearts, our emotions ran hot and cold, off and on. We swapped love notes in hallways, lingering looks across cafeteria tables and class rings. I suppose we both knew it wouldn't last but pretended it would, crafting names for our kids and careers that would allow us to travel. We parted ways the night of my first Jimmy Buffett concert: each of us leaving a piece of our soul with the other. There were others. Work girls and college girls and summer fun girls from the Chesapeake Bay. Now their tender words and hair ribbons lie wedged into a small cardboard box that remains almost forgotten... but not quiet.

I married the girl of my dreams. The shy, doll-eyed angel with the chipmunk cheeks and sundress tan who, for a time, thought I was cute and funny. When I said "I do," I did, but I sometimes wonder: Is it enough?

Oh, I don't question if she is enough. Of course she is. But am I enough? Have I been husband enough, father enough, lover enough? Have I provided, cherished, and honored enough.

Love may indeed blaze for a time with the passion of a mighty flame, but it is the golden embers of small coals that keep our feet warm and bed sacred.

Place me as a seal over your heart, my love. Rest your head on my shoulder and cling to my arm as we walk toward the blazing warmth of the setting sun. You are my mighty flame, the spark that ignites my spirit. Let us love and expire together in each other's arms.

Prayer

Precious Lord, I am your servant, laid before your feet to offer you praise and Glory for the almighty, majestic God you are.

Accept my praise; may your love blaze within me.

BUILDING BLOCKS OF FAITH

True love is friendship caught on fire. - *French proverb*

He Said, *She Said*

Journal

....
....
....
....
....
....
....
....
....
....
....
....
....
....
....
....
....
....
....
....
....
....
....
....
....
....
....
....
....
....

Sealed with a Kiss

She Said

Place me like a seal over your heart, like a seal on your arm; for love is as strong as death, its jealousy unyielding as the grave. It burns like blazing fire, like a mighty flame.

Song of Solomon 8:6

I've lost love once. But not to death: to divorce. I wondered if God would ever allow me an opportunity to know real love.

When my husband's dad died, we comforted his mother as she mourned her soul mate. She pressed her fingers against her lips, kissed them and touched the husk of her husband. "I'll see him again," she whispered, comforted in her belief. When her fingers touched his lips, she sealed that belief with a kiss.

I stared as my brother eased my mother into the backseat of his car. Mom kissed one finger and pointed it tenderly toward dad's casket. I knew the ache I felt couldn't compare to hers. He was her lifelong mate. Her kiss sealed him eternally as her own.

I wonder how God views the fleeting commitment of today's modern family. Instead of learning how to love in sickness, poverty and worst-case circumstance, "domestic partners" escape at the first signs of trouble.

Solomon had commitment issues to be sure. But the depth and intimacy of his writings on love suggest God's true passion for us and His burning desire for every marital relationship. Solomon's words testify to what love is - a holy bond sealed across our hearts.

Some years later I watched as my husband's mother took her final breaths. I leaned against Tim and whispered, "You know she's not coming back." He nodded. "She's not only seen God but she's seen your dad. She won't return."

I feel sure that was the truth. When the gates of heaven opened to welcome her home, part of her reward had to be the reunion of a lifetime...the one sealed with a kiss—her husband.

God did bless me with the love of my life. He opened my heart placed within it the desire, the passion and the understanding of real love—something deeper than the deepest emotion and more passionate than the sexual relationship. Each time I kiss my husband, I know that he is sealed in my heart and that he is my burning flame.

Does the one you love burn within you? God offered us the ability to know real love. He gave us the example. Trust your relationship to Him. Seal it with a kiss.

Prayer

Father, bring us closer to you. That is my hearts desire.

BUILDING BLOCKS OF FAITH

So heavy is the chain of wedlock that it needs two to carry it,

and sometimes three. *- Alexandre Dumas*

He Said, *She Said*

Journal

....
....
....
....
....
....
....
....
....
....
....
....
....
....
....
....
....
....
....
....
....
....
....
....
....
....
....
....
....

We Deserved More Time
He Said

Come, my lover, let us go to the countryside, let us spend
the night in the villages. Let us go early to the vineyards to
see if the vines have budded, if their blossoms have opened,
and if the pomegranates are in bloom—
there I will give you my love.

Song of Solomon 7:11-12 (NIV)

Dear, I'm sorry.

I meant what I said—oh those many years ago when I promised you the moon and stars and days filled with rich foods and sweet drink, but then came the hard work of making a living and honestly honey, how much of the world can we see with just two weeks of vacation each year. You understood. Of course you did. You were the frugal one, the one who set budgets and banked paychecks for unseen emergencies. So we shelved our travel plans, packing our dreams into folders marked "beach house," "Europe," and "Yosemite."

For a while we enjoyed weekends in cottages borrowed from friends. But the days were too few and besides, the boys needed us at scout meetings, on ball fields, and in the kitchen where you made our house a home. Here, look at this photo. Here you are sitting on the sea wall in St. Thomas. See that smile? See how, even with the glare of the tropical sun in your eyes, you're still beaming with that carefree smile that now sags, thin and pale.

There was hope for a time after the boys left for college, but then our parents became sick and then the grandkids... my God, think of them. Would you really have wanted to exchange their laughter and cooing for a few months in the vineyards of Tuscany?

Before I heard—before the oncologist called—I was dusting off those dreams. I wanted to see if we could recapture the magic we'd enjoyed oh those years ago. But now it's too late. Now there's only you and me and each day there is less of you.

Were we to leave right now it would be too late. So we won't. We'll stay right here in this room, on this bed, among the deepening shadows that diminish the light in your eyes. All that is left is the moon and stars and they are not enough.

Oh dear, I am sorry. Please forgive me. When you said I do, I didn't. I didn't take you to the pyramids and glaciers and mountaintops like I promised. You deserved more. You deserved the world.

We deserved more time.

Prayer

Lord, I ask that the power of a loving God would exhibit itself in peace and hope, in provision and in our relationship. Save us from ourselves... save us for You.

BUILDING BLOCKS OF FAITH

A successful marriage requires falling in love many times, always with the same person. - *Mignon McLaughlin*

He Said, *She Said*

Journal

"Time To..."

She Said

Come, my lover, let us go to the countryside, let us spend
the night in the villages. Let us go early to the vineyards to
see if the vines have budded, if their blossoms have opened,
and if the pomegranates are in bloom—
there I will give you my love.

Song of Solomon 7:11-12 NIV

Time is a killer. There never seems to be enough and when I held a job outside the home, plus my family, plus church, plus the ministry...there was even less.

My husband's a shift-worker and there were days I literally passed him on the road—him on his way to work, me on my way home. I hated that.

Finances and four growing sons dictated the circumstances of time more than our desire to be together. So, when stress made me sick, my husband and I had a real heart-to-heart.

"What's most important?" I asked. "The kids are grown and though it's far from great, we're in the best financial situation we've ever been in."

"I know," my husband agreed. "So if you want to resign your job, then do it. I do miss you."

And that...was all I needed to hear. Not the, "if you want to resign then do it" part; but the three words every woman wants to hear—"I miss you."

We'd spent the last 24 years struggling to provide for our family, digging from beneath mounds of medical expenses that nearly bankrupted us. What was wrong with spending quality time with the man I love? Selfish...maybe. But maybe not.

Solomon enticed his lover to spend time with him, to sneak off for a weekend getaway, accept his advances of love. He knew the importance of spending time with the woman he loved, wooing her, focusing his full attention on her and her on him. It solidified their relationship, bonded them—brought them closer.

I knew my plate was overflowing and my husband, kind and sweet, supported my tediously balanced plate. But when God called me into the ministry, into a different season of life with my husband, a decision had to be made.

These days my husband and I spend lots of time together. Well-meaning friends joked it wouldn't last; we'd grow tired of one another. Instead, we grow closer. We talk more, do things together, listen better, and desire each other more. He is my lover, my friend, my brother in Christ, and my soul mate, and I make every effort to spend quality time with him...now more than ever.

God instituted the marital relationship as a sacred and holy place—a place where one man and one woman can share their deepest, passionate love.

Make time to spend with the one you love. God blesses the hours we spend in love.

Prayer

Father, I praise you for the joy and love that you bring. I praise you because you are the Master of all things, the God of the Universe, the maker of mankind. Lord, you are almighty.

Thank you Lord, for this day of thanksgiving.

BUILDING BLOCKS OF FAITH

A dress that zips up the back will bring a husband and wife together. - *James H. Boren*

He Said, *She Said*

Journal

....
....
....
....
....
....
....
....
....
....
....
....
....
....
....
....
....
....
....
....
....
....
....
....
....
....
....
....
....

Making Love

He Said

Your stature is like that of the palm, and your breasts like clusters of fruit. I said, "I will climb the palm tree; I will take hold of its fruit." May your breasts be like the clusters of the vine, the fragrance of your breath like apples, and your mouth like the best wine.

Song of Solomon 7:7-9 (NIV)

I saved myself for marriage, but I wasn't a virgin. I'd leered, lusted and slept with women in my head long before I carried my bride to bed. Still do, sometimes. This temptation to roam—with my eyes, with my hands—is Man's curse and Eve's wound. Our ancestor, Adam, failed his mate, too. When Eve needed his strength and protection, he withdrew, cowered and covered his shame with blame. "That woman, she..."

The legacy lingers. "But my wife. She refuses...I married an angel; I sleep with a witch... There's nothing wrong with looking as long as you don't touch..." Slowly Eve retreats into her shell, convinced the lies whispered into her ears and stamped upon her broken heart are true. "I'm not pretty, not worth loving, not worth fighting for. He won't stay. They never do."

How can I convince my wife she is lovely? How can I break through the husk holding her heart and kiss the scars that mark my failures as a man, husband, and lover? How can I kill the Curse of Adam and become the warrior God shaped me to be?

I must die to self and live for her.

Love demands I risk rejection from her and reject all others for her. Love demands I advance, give her my strength, and pour myself into her. This is death. This is man's mission. This is making love.

Yes my love, you are beautiful. You see stretch marks; I see love lines born of birth. You see wrinkles; I see the familiar pattern of your smile. You see gray, age spots and rolls of skin; I see a crown of glory, tender hands that help and a body that envelops me in love.

Your shape is perfectly fitted to me.

You are worth loving, worth dying for. You are the crowning glory of Creation, the radiance of God, and my very life.

Come. Let us expire in each others arms and make that which is eternal: love.

Prayer

Oh Father, what an amazing sight. What beauty. When I didn't think your love could get any sweeter...it did. Thank you for my wife, life and your love!

BUILDING BLOCKS OF FAITH

Attitude is a little thing that makes a big difference.

- Winston Churchill

He Said, *She Said*

Journal

....
....
....
....
....
....
....
....
....
....
....
....
....
....
....
....
....
....
....
....
....
....
....
....
....
....
....
....
....
....

Bosom Buddies

She Said

Your stature is like that of the palm, and your breasts like
clusters of fruit. I said "I will climb the palm tree; I will
take hold of its fruit." May your breasts be like the clusters
of the vine, the fragrance of your breath like apples, and
your mouth like the best wine.

Song of Solomon 7:7-9

She cried into her hands. Sobbed. And my heart broke.

Therese was young and beautiful, in her early thirties. She had everything to look forward to—her sixth wedding anniversary, children, a great job. Until...

"He'll never look at me in the same light. Not after this. The doctor said even with reconstructive surgery there will still be huge scars." Therese pulled a tissue from the box as we waited for the nurse to wheel her into surgery. "We've always teased about being bosom buddies. Guess not anymore."

Her husband stood outside her door, biting his nails. Breast cancer had forced her into a double mastectomy. The fear that her husband would see her as a lesser woman haunted her.

36

"Don't be silly. Josh loves you. He's not 'skin deep'," I said.

"But look at me," she cried. "I've worked hard to maintain my looks for him. Now, I'm going to lose both breasts and be marred for the rest of my life. What if..."

My first response was to say, "At least you'll have your life." But I didn't. It's hard to understand, hard to comprehend the fear of cancer, much less the fear of losing the physical part that makes one a woman. I wanted to say something, but this was one time nothing was the best something I could say. So I placed my arms around her while she cried.

I've complained about my looks. Laughed at my aging, pear-shaped body, but I am fortunate that I have my body, despite its flaws. Oh, I've been the guilty wife who's asked my husband that loaded question, "Do I look fat in these jeans?" He sweetly smiles and nods (the safe route) and how ashamed I feel. How ungrateful I seemed—to have my health, to have my body...to have my husband desire me, love me, for what's inside...not out.

Solomon complimented his lover, reinforced his love for her, his longing for her and he didn't hesitate to tell her. Throughout the book, he not only expresses his physical attraction to her but his mental attraction as well.

Josh paced until the doctor gave him the okay to see Therese. When he entered her room, he tenderly rubbed her cheek with his knuckle. Tears streamed as he hovered over her semi-conscious body; and when he pressed his head gently against her chest, he whispered, "I love you. We're always gonna be bosom buddies. Thank God, I still have you."

God gifted man and woman with the sexual experience, but what fuels the real experience is not the body, but the love beneath it...to have and to hold, in sickness and in health, for richer or for poorer for better, for worse, in sadness and in joy... to be bosom buddies, forsaking all others, for as long as you both shall live.

The challenge in the vows is demanding. Love your spouse. Take the vow.

Prayer

Father, I pray your loving hand over us. I offer you my praise for the love you give to me. Thank you lord for the blessings of this day. You are almighty.

BUILDING BLOCKS OF FAITH

Cancer is a word, not a sentence. - *John Diamond*

He Said, *She Said*

Journal

Stinky Feet

He **S**aid

Jesus said, "Let the little children come to me, and do not hinder them, for the kingdom of heaven belongs to such as these."

Matthew 19:14 NIV

I was married in Saint Marks Church at the age of five. The pastor's son performed the ceremony in the basement of the sanctuary. I didn't ask the bride's father for permission, but he didn't seem upset by the news that his only daughter was getting married. I think he was just happy that she was finally potty trained.

Our wedding rings were large and ornate things cut from a brown grocery bag. We were trying to make a social statement and that statement was, "The pre-school class wants more craft projects and fewer scripture memorization lessons!"

We concluded the ceremony by doing what most couples do on their wedding night. We got naked—at least, from the knees down. I helped Peggy out of her shoes and socks, then kicked off my sneakers. Next, we sat on the floor and smelled each other's feet.

We were Methodist. Baptists would never think of doing such a thing. I'm pretty sure they forbid the touching of toes, too.

The marriage didn't last, though. I forget why. It may have had something to do with different nap times.

But, for a few hours at least, we threw caution, not to mention our shoes, to the wind. That's how kids are. They do crazy things like believe in Cinderella stories and Piggy Toes, and that new crayons are cool and adults aren't.

I think that's one reason Christ said, "Let the little children come to me." He was tired of eating with the adults. He wanted to sit with the girls and boys and throw cake, pop balloons and laugh until His sides hurt.

It's a scary thing to think the Kingdom of God belongs to kids, but that's what He said. Perhaps what He really meant was that the Kingdom of God belongs to those who seek adventure, love smelly feet and long to run through the halls of the King's castle.

What dour duty keeps you from sharing in your Master's joy? God desires our love, not our duty. Isn't it time you cast off your shoes, ran barefoot through the grass, and played footsie with your Lord?

Prayer

Lord, bless me today with your Spirit of freedom, wisdom and wonder.

BUILDING BLOCKS OF FAITH

Outwardly we are wasting away, but inwardly we are renewed each day by the Spirit of Christ.

He Said, *She Said*

Journal

....
....
....
....
....
....
....
....
....
....
....
....
....
....
....
....
....
....
....
....
....
....
....
....
....
....
....
....
....
....
....
....

A Mom's Angst

She Said

Jesus said, "Let the little children come to me, and do not hinder them, for the kingdom of heaven belongs to such as these."

Matthew 19:14 NIV

We stood staring at the Credit Union computer. A picture of our son, standing in front of an ATM, filled the bank executive's monitor.

"Do you know this man?" he asked, tapping the screen.

My husband's shoulders shook as the color drained from his face. With his knuckles resting on the desk, Tim nodded. Then he stepped back and leaned against the wall. I thought, "Thank God. At least the boy had the good sense to steal from his brother's checking account and not from a stranger."

A prodigal child isn't that unusual. The more I talk to others, the more I find that most every family has one. Still that day it felt like we were the only ones in the world with a child who'd gone awry. This boy, the youngest of four, had drifted down a dangerous path and it seemed as if there was nothing we could do to stop it.

I'm not sure anyone can imagine the dull ache that lingers when a child rejects what is right and chooses the wrong path. "Tough love, that's what he needs," well-meaning friends said. "Press charges. Kick him out. It's for his own good."

We didn't. Two years passed. He never came back.

Then last winter, as I stood by my mother-in-law's casket, I caught a glimpse of a tall, slender man with shoulder-length hair and a beard. Whispers filled the chapel as those in the receiving line asked, "Is that him? The grandson that went missing?" My husband ran to our son and wrapped his arms around him.

Christ said, "Let the little children come to me, and do not hinder them." Prison bars hinder. Addictions hinder. Pride and shame hinder kids from returning home.

Jesus called the children to His side. He healed, taught and touched them. When His disciples tried to push the children away, Jesus pulled them close.

Our prodigal son wandered off after his grandmother's funeral for who knows where. But we rest in the assurance that he's safe in the hands of Christ. We have hope in that promise. And we pray and trust that someday God will lead him back to the arms of a loving Savior who is ready to forgive and restore.

If you see our son wandering the streets, do not judge him by the way he looks or for what he's done. Just send him home, please.

Prayer

Allow us the courage to practice tough love, then comfort us
through the process.

BUILDING BLOCKS OF FAITH

There is truth in "no pain, no gain." Strength comes through
the trials.

He Said, *She Said*

Journal

....
....
....
....
....
....
....
....
....
....
....
....
....
....
....
....
....
....
....
....
....
....
....
....
....
....
....
....
....
....
....
....
....

She Won't Shut Up
He Said

There is a time for everything, and a season for every activity under the heavens, a time to tear and a time to mend, a time to be silent and a time to speak.

Ecclesiastes 3:1, 7 NIV

When it comes to talking men are at a serious disadvantage. Experts tell us that women speak, on average, 20,000 words a day. Men might utter 20. We process information, calculate our response and carefully weigh the impact of our words. Often we do this in front of the TV.

Let's say, for example, that your wife asks if the new pair of jeans she bought makes her look fat. If you're like most married men, you may have some vague idea that a conversation is about to transpire that could seriously damage your marriage, not to mention your ear drums, so you run to the garage. But suppose, as you open the door and step into the pantry, you remember that you don't have a garage. Well this would be a good time to keep quiet.

He Said, *She Said*

The writer of Ecclesiastes didn't have cable or TV but he did have 700 wives and 300 concubines, so in addition to having some serious dinner conflicts come Valentine's Day, he also struggled to find a quite place to read the sports section. This may explain why Solomon spent so much time writing things in his journal like, "Wife 587 is talking again. Oh God, can't you make it stop?" This may also explain the origins of the garage.

If there's one thing we can learn from the wisest king on earth it's that there is a time to speak and time to remain silent. A few centuries later when the King of Kings was asked if the woman caught in adultery should be stoned, Christ kept quiet. When he was arrested, beaten and sentenced to death for a crime he did not commit, Jesus remained silent. When mocked and encouraged to call on His Father and save himself, our Lord refused. I'm not suggesting marriage is anywhere near as excruciating as a slow death on the cross. Okay, maybe just a little on the days when I have to vacuum, dust and fold the laundry.

But I am saying that when it comes to verbal communication, Solomon provided wise council and Christ a good example to follow. Everyone needs to be noticed, understood and heard. We all need more affirmation and less confrontation. So compliment—don't criticize—and if you can't say something nice, keep your mouth shut. Or at least hide in the garage.

He Said, *She Said*

Prayer

Lord, help me to see my bride with your eyes and love her with your heart.

BUILDING BLOCKS OF FAITH

Home is where the heart is, and my heart is the arms of my wife.

He Won't Open Up

She Said

There is a time for everything, and a season for every activity under the heavens, a time to tear and a time to mend, a time to be silent and a time to speak.

Ecclesiastes 3:1, 7 NIV

I peeked around the door into the living room and saw my husband staring through, not at, the television, his brow furrowed. Obviously he had more on his mind than his team's injured quarterback hobbling off the field. The network cut to a commercial, so I walked to the couch, wrapped my arms around him and buried my face into the fold of his neck. He shifted his weight and leaned away.

"Is it my breath or are you mad at me?"

"Just trying to watch the game."

"But it's a commercial."

He shrugged and continued to stare at an ad for fabric softener. I snuggled next to him and asked what happened to the player...was he out for good or just a few plays. My husband reached for the remote and changed the channel. *Awkward.*

I asked his opinion of the election, how things were going at work, and if he'd given any more thought to our travel plans for Christmas. He glared at me with dead eyes, "Not now, Cin. I'm not in the mood."

Not in the mood? To talk? He has a mood for that?

I understand women converse on a whole different level than men. When it comes to talking, we have more gears than a logging truck. But I also know that solitude can be deadly, isolation the first step toward depression. Given enough time, what begins as a sulk grows into a full-blown funk.

I mentioned my husband's foul mood to a co-worker. He said I should give my spouse some space; that sometimes guys just have to think things through. I decided it was pretty lame advice from a guy with a college degree and most of his teeth, but I took his advice and kept quite. I didn't prod, push or ask what was wrong...I just let him brood.

I still don't know what bothered my husband that week. He never said. I don't think it was anything I did, but I'm a wife, so when he's in a bad mood I assume it's my fault. I wish he would open up, share his feelings and expose his heart the way I long to share mine with him. But he's just a guy who's not so much tall as he is handsome and quiet.

The wisdom of Solomon directed us that there is a time for everything under the sun—a time to speak and a time to be silent.

I suppose this was my time to be silent. And as hard as it was... it was good advice.

If he wants to talk, I'll listen. If he wants to walk it off, I'll hike behind him. And if he just wants to be loved and left alone, I can do that, too. The important thing is that I heard him say "I do." If my husband never says another word to me, he's said enough.

Prayer

Father, help me to understand the value of silence and peace.

BUILDING BLOCKS OF FAITH

There is peace in silence and respect in allowing it.

My Weaker Vessel Leaks

He Said

Likewise, ye husbands, dwell with them according to knowl-edge, giving honor unto the wife, as unto the weaker vessel, and as being heirs together of the grace of life; that your prayers be not hindered.

1 Peter 3:7 KJV

My weaker vessel leaks. Not much, but enough to concern me. I think perhaps her planking is loose. This would be unfortunate because she is such a beautiful vessel. Why I can go for days just watching her and have, only after a while she tells me to stop staring. I think my vessel has a streak of modesty running through her ribs.

Soon after we first met I dreamed of taking her to places like Tahiti, Bora-Bora and Cancun, but lately she only wants to go to the mall, her parent's or the grocery store. When I suggest that such ports are boring, she thinks I mean she's boring and she starts leaking.

But not in front of me. Instead, I have to discover this for myself. Sometimes the evidence will be on her pillow, wadded up with tissues in the wastebasket.

I thought surrounding her with a fleet of smaller looking vessels might help, so I suggested she make a few, which she did, but this only caused her to leak more. Sometimes she'll leak right in front of the smaller vessels. I'm sure this scares them.

The development and delivery of these smaller vessels took a great toll on her. Her lines became hardened, her brow fixed in a glare. It changed her in other ways, too. My weaker vessel used to have a classic, petit stern, so carefully sculpted that other men on the docks would stop and stare. This no longer happens, which is fine by me, but my weaker vessel seems to miss the attention. She's forever looking at her reflection in the water and sighing.

A few weeks ago, I found her standing in front of a mirror inspecting some bumps on her hull. I told her not to be concerned; that they were probably barnacles and that's what comes from a seasoned vessel. Of course, she leaked. Then she locked herself in the bathroom.

A short time later, one of our two tiny vessels rushed into the room asking if something was wrong with the mother ship. I told him she was leaking again, but not to worry. She'd be out shortly to fix dinner. She emerged a few minutes later listing to one side, but not on the side closest to my arm.

I don't know how I ended up with such a frail vessel, but I'm glad I did. All I know to do is hold her close, keep a weather eye out for storms and ignore the changing shape of her hull.

Tomorrow I might take her to the mall so I can buy her a new suit of sails. We might swing by her parent's house, too. I need to keep my weaker vessel happy and afloat. Without her, I'd drown.

Prayer

Lord, guard our hearts, marriage and family.

BUILDING BLOCKS OF FAITH

Vessels come in all shapes, but without love, care and devotion

He Said, *She Said*

Journal

....
....
....
....
....
....
....
....
....
....
....
....
....
....
....
....
....
....
....
....
....
....
....
....
....
....
....
....
....
....
....

each will break apart and sink.

Weaker Vessel, My Keel!

She Said

*Likewise, ye husbands, dwell with them according to knowl-
edge, giving honor unto the wife, as unto the weaker vessel,
and as being heirs together of the grace of life;
that your prayers be not hindered.*

1 Peter 3:7 KJV

Weaker vessel, my keel! Who does he thinks gets us from point A to B? It's certainly not him. He won't even look at a chart, much less ask for directions. Let's face it, gals, we keep the ship's log, the galley stocked and the crew in clean laundry. If we are the weaker vessel, it's because we're worn out from slaving under such a heavy load.

I love being a wife and mother, but my responsibilities take a toll, leaving me tired and worn out. When I lay down at night my mind never shuts down. If one of my family is sick or dealing with a problem, I worry. As the nervous nurturer, I'm always trying to solve their problems, but sometimes I just want to be cared for. I need to be pampered, appreciated and reminded that the home work I do matters.

I long for the security of his strong arm wrapped around me, the firmness of his shoulder beneath my cheek. I need him to hold my hand the way he clutches the remote and to pay as much attention to me as he does *Sports Center*.

God made Eve sensitive, compassionate and caring. Our weakness is our tenderness, so when we're in tune to the needs of others we hurt, too. My hubby knows to trust my woman's intuition because it's God's gift to the weaker vessel, His back channel to our heart.

And into the heart of my husband.

When I purr, he pursues. When I cry, he melts. When I am weak, he is strong, rushing to protect and provide. I may be the weaker vessel, but I control the rudder and together we are unsinkable.

God has honored woman with the responsibility of caring for her man. Most of the men I know wouldn't even wear matching socks if it weren't for a wife sorting the clean laundry. Our weakness lifts us to a place of honor, so ladies, don't begrudge your calling or take offense at your rank. God has shaped us with a tender heart for His purpose.

Be strong in other ways, gain wisdom and knowledge. Seek success, but submit to the Lord and leave room for His love. Only then can you transport your family to the throne of Christ.

Prayer

Father, help us to set a course for purity, love and pleasant
passages.

BUILDING BLOCKS OF FAITH

A godly husband needs trust, respect and encouragement. Love

He Said, *She Said*

Journal

....
....
....
....
....
....
....
....
....
....
....
....
....
....
....
....
....
....
....
....
....
....
....
....
....
....
....
....
....
....
....
....
....

him in this way and he will take you to the ends of the earth.

Can't Get Enough of Her, Ah…Cooking

He Said

The husband should fulfill his marital duty to his wife, and likewise the wife to her husband. The wife does not have authority over her own body but yields it to her husband. In the same way, the husband does not have authority over his own body but yields it to his wife.

Do not deprive each other.

1 Corinthians 7: 4-5 NIV

Boy do I enjoy my wife's, ah…cooking. Some days, that's all I think about. But I've found she's not all that fond of food, which is surprising giving how much time she spends basting by the pool. It's like she wants me to notice but not nibble, you know? The other night I tried to sneak a taste, but she slapped my hand away.

"But I haven't eaten in weeks," I said.

"And you're not going to now. It's late, you'll make a mess and I'm not in the mood."

He Said, She Said

If I had my way, my I'd eat three meals a day with snacks in between. My wife calls this gluttony. I call it a healthy diet. The other day I complained to my pastor about my wife's skimpy servings. I mentioned Paul's letter to the church in Corinth, thinking that he'd be impressed with my Biblical knowledge, but he only wanted to know why I was behind on my tithing. These pastors, sometimes it's like they have a one track mind. Anyway, when I explained that I hadn't had a decent meal in months, he said I should be grateful—that his wife put him on a diet years ago. He's an old guy with bad teeth and no hair, so I can't blame her, but still I didn't leave his office encouraged.

Occasionally I'll see my neighbor's wife grilling on the patio. I know I shouldn't look, but a hungry man is a desperate man. Bob Marley said this I think. Or maybe it was Bob Dylan. I'm sure it was a man. I'd never steal another man's meal because that's just wrong, but it's hard to keep your appetite in check when the media and sports bars offer free appetizers.

The Bible says Jesus was a man, just like me, who faced the same temptations I face. I don't know how he could, since they didn't have *Baywatch* back then, but that's a doctrinal discussion for another day. Still, forty days is a long time. And when He was tempted to turn rocks into bread, he refused. There are a lot of things I could say about taking matters into your own hands here, but I won't.

What I will say is that I made a vow to my bride. I promised to honor, cherish and love her till death do us part which, in my case, will probably be from malnutrition.

Look, some days call for a feast, others a snack. Both can satisfy our nutritional needs for physical affection, so share up the food, wives! And men don't forget to wash before dinner and say "thanks" when you're done.

Prayer

Father, help me to keep my heart pure, eyes chaste and hands to myself. Wait, that didn't sound right. What I meant was, help me to keep my hands on my wife. No... oh, never mind.

BUILDING BLOCKS OF FAITH

There's a reason they call it "making love" and not "making out" or "making do."

Journal

....
....
....
....
....
....
....
....
....
....
....
....
....
....
....
....
....
....
....
....
....
....
....
....
....
....
....
....
....
....
....
....

Keep Your Hands Off My Cookies

She Said

The husband should fulfill his marital duty to his wife, and likewise the wife to her husband. The wife does not have authority over her own body but yields it to her husband. In the same way, the husband does not have authority over his own body but yields it to his wife.

Do not deprive each other.

1 Corinthians 7: 4-5 NIV

I'm not the swiftest cook, but my man's never gone hungry, so when I go to all the trouble to wash, peel and sauté my, ah...forbidden fruit, it would be nice if he'd show a little appreciation—or table manners.

The other night I was in the mood for "fundue." This happens sometimes. Not often and certainly not when the kids are around, but there I was lighting the burner, stirring the pot and peeling the wrappers off chocolate. When I get in the mood

66

to cook, I go all out. It's a gourmet affair, not some fast food pit stop at a drive through window.

Just then, my husband had a snack attack and stole one of my kisses. I slapped his hand and told him to wait until I was ready. He strolled back into the living room to watch TV because that's what little boys do when things don't go their way. They pout. In a few minutes, the flame died and the "fundue" hardened.

I hope I'm not being too bold when I say this, but I think my husband would eat garbage if I'd let him. He just doesn't show any discretion when it comes to quality cuisine. The other night I caught him browsing the Internet for junk food. Do you think he was embarrassed? He was not. He said all men do it. I don't think that's true, but even if they do, I wish my husband would show a little more taste. Or at least discretion.

I'll be the first to admit that I'm a finicky eater. I get worn out keeping the kids fed, bathed and from killing each other. I work days at a job that pays too little and nights cleaning a house that's too messy. So when it comes to meeting the physical needs of my husband's appetite, most nights I'm just plum tuckered out.

I understand that he needs to eat a lot and often. God knows I try. But I have needs, too, and one of them is to be left alone when I'm not in the mood to cook. To be honest, most evenings I'd rather take a cup of coffee and plate of cookies onto the front porch and talk. Not every meal has to end with a grunt, sigh and belch.

Sometimes less is more, so men, give us time to grow in our desire. You may find that the waiting makes the meal more filling.

Prayer

Honestly, Lord, there are times when...you know, he is more job than joy. Help me to trust you to clean him up, slow down and teach him to turn out the lights?

BUILDING BLOCKS OF FAITH

Love under covers is messy, loud and fun.

He Said, *She Said*

Journal

....
....
....
....
....
....
....
....
....
....
....
....
....
....
....
....
....
....
....
....
....
....
....
....
....
....
....
....
....
....

She's Still the One

He Said

Samson said to his father, "Get her for me.
She's the right one for me."

Judges 14:3 NIV

I received an e-mail from a friend today. He said his bride moved out last weekend. This was his third marriage. Apparently, the third time was not the charm. One thing seems certain, though. She wasn't the right one for him.

I met my wife at a stop light in Palm Beach Florida. She was cute, tanned and had all her teeth—a feature that immediately made her a novelty in my family. One look at her and I knew I'd found the right one. I don't know what she thought of me and now, thirty years later, I'm still too afraid to ask.

Samson thought he'd found the right one, too. When he returned to the town of Timnah, he told his parents, "I have seen a Philistine woman, now get her for me as my wife."

Like good Jewish parents they replied, "What? Are there no good girls among our people that you should go to the uncircumcised Philistines for a wife? God forbid that you should look with favor upon your uncle's daughter Eunice."

"She has the face of a goat."

"Ah, but behind the flap of your tent in the dark of the new moon is not the milk of a goat a thing to savored?"

"Just get me the young Philistine woman, Mom."

Like my friend, Samson's marriage barely lasted through the honeymoon. It turns out Ellen DeGeneres speaks not only for *Cover Girl* magazine, but for Samson, too, when she boasts that, "Inner beauty is important. . .but not nearly as important as outer beauty."

Spray-on tans and cosmetics are skin deep, but beauty goes clear to the soul. That kind of loveliness can't be appreciated in a one night hook-up. You have to get to know the person, see them at their worst, and hold them when they break. Then, maybe you'll begin to see the radiance of their character.

I don't know if my wife was the only one for me or just the right one to put up with me, but one thing's for sure. Knowing that she'd already given her heart to Christ made it easier for me to marry her. Now, when I'm cold, condescending and careless, I know He's loving her in the way I won't. And I know, too, that she'll be waiting for me when I grow into the kind of husband she deserves.

Prayer

Father, help us grow old together.

BUILDING BLOCKS OF FAITH

Old goats have lots of kids and years of memories.

He Said, *She Said*

Journal

....
....
....
....
....
....
....
....
....
....
....
....
....
....
....
....
....
....
....
....
....
....
....
....
....
....
....
....
....
....

Mr. "Not Right Now"

She Said

Samson said to his father, "Get her for me.
She's the right one for me."

Judges 14:3 NIV

The coin spun end over end as I flipped it from my fingers. Heads, I go out with this guy, tails, I don't. It wasn't like you had to take a ticket to get a date with me. My schedule was fairly flexible—okay, really flexible.

The fifty-cent piece sailed above my head and my friend Leza snatched it out of the air.

"Stop being silly! This isn't a game. He's the guy. He's Mr. Right."

She slammed the coin down. I picked it up and flipped it again. *Shoot. Heads.*

I crawled into the Volkswagen bug, barely able to close the door, and we raced off to a diner. My lucky Mr. Right ordered fish. His favorite. Apparently he thought it was mine, too. (Just for the record, I think fish belong in the sea, stream or aquarium, not on my plate).

He drove me to his parent's home, escorted me through the "hall of fame" where every award he'd accumulated since prekindergarten was displayed—including his first baby tooth. The night ended abruptly when he leaned close and said, "You know you'd like nothing better than to spend the night with me."

"Yeah, right!" I laughed in his face and marched out. As I walked home (yes, I walked home), I recalled the coin toss and Leza's advice that this was "Mr. Right." Instead of Mr. Right, my date was the epitome of "Mr. Not Right Now...or ever!"

Choosing a mate, or even a date, is tough. I know. I've dated some duds and suffered through a failed marriage. Too often my desires weren't pure, or my decisions wise. I chose without the discernment of the Father—letting luck, circumstances and outward appearances dictate my decisions.

After a failed marriage, I ask God, *help me choose.* He matched me with an unlikely mate. My husband's quiet; I yap. He's low key; I'm high octave, bordering on shrill. But we are what God desires, a couple that compliments one another.

Trusting God for a mate may mean learning to rejoice in who you are while you wait. That beats taking a gamble on Mr. Wrong. Be wise, be discerning and seek to find someone who will cradle your heart with the tender touch of God.

Lord, if He's the right one for me. Go and get him for me. I trust you.

Prayer

Father, I trust you to lead me in a decision for a life-mate.

BUILDING BLOCKS OF FAITH

Journal

....
....
....
....
....
....
....
....
....
....
....
....
....
....
....
....
....
....
....
....
....
....
....
....
....
....
....
....
....
....
....
....

What's Not to Like?

Why lick the spoon when you can scrape the bowl?

He Said

Then he went down and talked with the woman,
and he liked her.

Judges 14:7 NIV

He went. He saw. He liked. Yes, this pretty much describes the way men pick-up women.

Oh I know, you'd like to think that we men are a little more discerning, that we want to know you as a person or at least if you can speak in complete sentences. But this is not important for men. Not at first, anyway.

Let's say there's a guy, who we'll call Elmer, and he's out with some guy friends. Across the room is a voluptuous blonde in a short skirt wearing a spandex tube top that's stretched way beyond the fabric's tensile strength. Her name is Tina. Tina's skin is baked golden brown from repetitive trips to a tanning salon and her naturally brown hair is bleached to the color of honey.

Sitting next to Tina is her best friend, Hilda. Hilda is wearing a one-piece jumper that appears to be made from an old army tent. Her face, in color and texture, looks like the surface of the moon and on her head is what appears to be a hat made from a very large rodent. Perhaps a gopher or Canadian hockey player. On closer inspection, Elmer realizes this is Hilda's hair.

Now, who do you think Elmer is going to ask out? This question is for you women. We men already know the answer.

It doesn't matter that Hilda is a nuclear physicist with a degree in advanced molecular quantum physics and has, in fact, actually walked on the surface of the moon. She could be the head of the United Nations, and have actually developed an alternative fuel derived from Styrofoam packing peanuts. It doesn't matter to Elmer.

That's because later that evening, while sitting on the sofa in his tiny apartment, Elmer will fantasize about how Tina almost said "yes" and would have, except the words "drop dead" came out of her mouth first. He'll also picture the two of them frolicking in a hot tub together. This is unfortunate because at the same time Elmer is thinking about a girl he'll never date, Hilda will be sitting in her small apartment thinking that Elmer is really cute.

"If he'd have just said hello, and given me a chance," she'll say while eating Cheese Whiz straight from the can, "he'd see my inner beauty."

In a perfect a world, Elmer and Hilda would meet, date, marry and raise a litter of hairy hockey playing girls. But life isn't fair. It's fractured by sin.

Men look at the outside, rarely seeing the heart of a woman the way God does. Perhaps if men took the time to talk more and lust less, we'd find the inner beauty buried beneath the Cheese Whiz. It worked for Samson, Abraham and Jacob. Maybe it'll work for you, too, mister.

Prayer

Father, help me to look past the skin and into her soul.

BUILDING BLOCKS OF FAITH

She can't say "no" if you don't ask.

He Said, *She Said*

Journal

....
....
....
....
....
....
....
....
....
....
....
....
....
....
....
....
....
....
....
....
....
....
....
....
....
....
....
....
....
....
....
....

Yes (X) or No ( )

She Said

*Then he went down and talked with the woman,
and he liked her.*

Judges 14:7 NIV

I really liked him...a lot. His green eyes and beautiful smile were unforgettable. The problem was that he didn't know I existed.

Third grade was tough, and my blue cat-eye reading glasses with lenses as thick as a cola bottle didn't exactly rate me *Miss Popularity*. I had a crush on Barry and talking to him was out of the question. My throat just shriveled shut. So I dreamed.

I watched my friend, Mary, scribble a note to her heart-throb, Jason. He sat six desks behind her, third row from the window. She squirmed in her seat, batting her eyes in hopes he'd catch her flirting. Mary neatly proclaimed her heartfelt feelings for Jason on a sheet of notebook paper.

Do you like me? Check one. Yes ( ) No ( )

She folded the page then passed it down the aisle to Jason.

He smiled and opened the note, grabbed his number 2 pencil, and drew a heavy black **X** over the **Yes** box.

Huh, I thought. *It's that easy?* Later, I penned my heart's message and then, standing against the lunchroom wall, took a deep breath. I slipped the note into his hand, my face crimson and heart racing. *He'd like me if he'd just take time to talk to me.*

Do you like me? Yes ( ) No ( )

Barry read the note then dropped it in the huge trashcan a few feet away. I should've known better. I hid behind a cinder block column, broken-hearted. "No" really hurt.

Samson didn't have to write a note. He forged ahead proclaiming his affections to the girl of his dreams. (She must've been attracted by his pecs and abs). But he saw what he liked and went after her.

I don't write notes these days, but when I read scripture, I see more than chapters and verses. My eyes focus on the words Christ carefully crafted. Love letters written for me.

God likes me...better yet, He loves me. He knows I stammer when I talk, yet He wants to chat—tell me how much He likes me. Even when I drop His notes in the trash barrel, He writes continually, until I see His desire to know me.

Today I opened my Bible and pushed my finger down the pages recounting Christ's sacrifice. Suddenly, at the bottom of the page, words faded into view.

*Do you like me? Yes (**X**) or No ( )*

That's enough to mend my heart and lure me from behind the cinder block column.

Prayer

Lord, help me to see the beauty within myself.

BUILDING BLOCKS OF FAITH

Strive to see the beauty in others.

He Said, She Said
Journal

Cry Baby

He Said

*Then Samson's wife threw herself on him, sobbing, "You
hate me! You don't really love me...." She cried the whole
seven days of the feast. So on the seventh day he finally told
her, because she continued to press him.*

Judges 14:16-17 NIV

A few years ago a friend offered to give a very large sum
of money to his church. In exchange, he wanted a seat on the
finance committee. He had some strong opinions on church
growth, the minister's preaching and the types of worship
services offered. The finance committee declined his gift. Now,
years later, the church still lacks adequate parking, sufficient
seating in the sanctuary and enough cribs, rockers and Legos in
the nursery and pre-school classes.

What it doesn't lack is integrity. Their allegiance to God and
His leading was firmly established when the finance committee
refused to be bought. A gift with strings attached is still a bribe.

When my boys were young, they would sometimes cry to

get their way. It didn't work. I'm old school, as was my father. So when they pitched a fit, I pitched them into "time out." My boys aren't married, yet, so I don't know what my stance will be with grandkids, but I'd like to think that I'm man enough to withstand a barrage of tears from a toddler.

I know with women, I'm not. I learned early in high school that weeping was the weapon of choice for girls. Every time I tried to break up with whomever I was going steady with, the girl would cry. Well, almost every time. Sherry Johnson applauded. But tears tear me down, make me weak and leave me apologizing for being so hard-hearted.

Samson was a man's man. He was Schwarzenegger, Rambo and Rocky all in one. He slew lions with his bare hands and slaughtered men with the jawbone of an ass, and yet he couldn't resist the tears of a woman. Love, even conditional love, seems appealing. But when we exchange our strength for affection, influence and affluence, we become slaves to a god with a little 'g.'

Thank God my wife doesn't use tears to get her way. And thank God He doesn't allow my tears to change His mind, either. My heavenly Father loves me too much to be swayed by my petty pleading, emotional outbursts and child-like games of "He loves me, He loves me not." No, that question was decided on the cross. He Loves me. Period.

Who are you trying to control through tears, nagging and

emotional guilt? Try love. It works wonders.

Prayer

Lord, give me the peace that comes with crying on your
shoulder.

BUILDING BLOCKS OF FAITH

Laugh and the world laughs with you. Cry and the coach yanks

He Said, *She Said*

Journal

you off the field.

Whine, Wine, Wean

She Said

Then Samson's wife threw herself on him, sobbing, "You hate me! You don't really love me...." She cried the whole seven days of the feast. So on the seventh day he finally told her, because she continued to press him.

Judges 14:16-17 NIV

I'd told him everything. Spilled my guts. And he wouldn't share a thing. It wasn't fair. Matt was a nice guy. We'd known each other for years, but when he came to me, using my shoulder to lean on, I never dreamed we'd be more than just friends. So when we began to date, I expected the same frank honesty about his feelings as I'd shared with him. Wrong.

Soon after we met, he'd asked me about my ex. I was tight-lipped, not wanting to open up. But I did. Women do. As we spent time together, I shared little things about that failed relationship. But every time I asked about his history, he sidestepped my questions.

"Why won't you tell me what happened to you?" I asked.

"You don't wanna know."

Wrong, again. Rule number one, guys. Never tell a woman she doesn't want to know. We always want to know. We're naturally inquisitive creatures. We share our hearts and expect the same in return. The strong silent type is for Hollywood. Give me a man with a pulse.

When Matt wouldn't talk, I did what women do. I cried. Still his lips were sealed. I wanted to know what brought him to me, a single mom with two small children. So I asked...and asked.

Samson's wife asked, too. Though her motives were different, the means to the end were the same. She hounded and nagged and then when that didn't work, she wept. Tears tear a man apart. We women know this.

It may not be fair. No...wait. All is fair in love. I suppose we could blame Eve. Once she bit into that fruit, she gained all sorts of knowledge, including how to mold a man and manipulate him. And though I chuckle a little at the thought of Eve nagging Adam, tearing up and saying, "I know why you won't eat what I've fixed for dinner. You don't love me. You hate me!"

Nagging. It's sinful. It's hurtful. It's ungodly. And it's exactly what Satan did to Eve.

Whining, nagging and getting our way may give us a sense of control, but it destroys the trust and bond between a man and women. In the end, her nagging cost her and Samson their marriage.

I paid a price, too. When I finally managed to manipulate Matt into opening up, he confessed that my friendship was the result of a bet. His buddies had bet $20 he couldn't get me to fall for him.

Gals, love your men and respect their silence. Be Godly women. Strengthen the value of the relationship by calming the urge to push, press and plead. It may be that his silence is the sweetest thing he never says.

Prayer

Oh God, we can be so sinful, so deceitful and unfair. Help me to be rational in my approach to others.

BUILDING BLOCKS OF FAITH

The best relationships are forged in trust

What A Heifer

He **S**aid

Samson said to them, "If you had not plowed with my heifer, you would not have solved my riddle."...Burning with anger, he returned to his father's home. And Samson's wife was given to one of his companions who had attended him at the feast.

Judges 14:18-20 NIV

I've dated some duds, but never a heifer. Oh, there was one girl in college. A sorority sister named Brenda. She was nowhere near what you might call a prize-winning 4-H cow, but I did need a cattle prod to keep her off me. While rubbing her bare foot against the back of my calve, she sang a popular Billy Joel song, emphasizing the words "Brenda and Eddie were still going steady in the summer of '75." I didn't see the need to explain to her that the year was 1976, not '75, or that we were not going steady and never would. Brenda was, after all, much too lazy.

I'm not even sure why I told that story.

Oh, right. Now I remember. Brenda was a farm girl and knew a thing or two about heifers. She told me about how, growing up in Pender County, she'd seen sights that a city boy like me couldn't possibly see. Sights like her cousin Junior riding naked down the middle of Highway 117 on her dad's best sow, her uncle Willie with his hand caught in the blades of a tobacco harvester, and how large hail from a summer storm can cause a grown man to cry. I learned a little about farming from Brenda and a lot about sororities.

For example, I learned that you couldn't date two girls from the same sorority ever. I found this out after I invited one of Brenda's "sisters" to a Kenny Loggins concert. Brenda's anger burned against me. She mixed metaphors using barnyard slang to describe my ancestral history. She ran home to her daddy.

Some days later, I heard that Brenda had brought her dad's banders back to the sorority house. Banders, if you don't know, are used to remove small but vital parts from boy cows. Upon hearing that, I moved on to greener pastures.

Betrayal, even if accidental, can be fatal. When Samson's wife betrayed his confidence, she picked her father's love over her husband's. Trust, devotion and forgiveness are vital to any relationship, especially our relationship with Christ.

Judas betrayed Jesus and died from his guilt. Peter promised he wouldn't, but did and wept because of it. Even I, in my own way, plow with another's heifer every time I pick the satisfaction of sin over the companionship of Christ.

Christ does not lack for company. If we refuse His love, He'll find another. It is we who remain isolated, alone and starved for companionship. Today if you are tempted to solve your problems through sin and treachery, stop and ask Christ to be the solution to your situation.

Prayer

Lord, when I'm tempted to fix my problems alone, hold my hands...behind my back.

BUILDING BLOCKS OF FAITH

Giving into sin is just another way of giving up on God.

Walk this Way

She Said

Samson said to them, "If you had not plowed with my heifer, you would not have solved my riddle."...Burning with anger, he returned to his father's home. And Samson's wife was given to one of his companions who had attended him at the feast.

Judges 14:18-20 NIV

He walked away and I never had the chance to explain.

I've always had the personality of a "pleaser," which often brought me heartache. Sixth grade was no exception. My creativity led me to "part-time" friends, whose superficial eyes judged me on looks and not my heart—eager for my help and quick to drop me when done.

Jimmy was different. He wore glasses, too. Thick black plastic frames—we had that in common and it wasn't long before we forged a nifty friendship. So when he invited me to help paint his soapbox derby car, I was thrilled.

We sketched and colored pictures of the wooden car, settling on navy blue with white flames on the hood. If Jimmy didn't win the race, he'd have the coolest car in the derby.

Ted Martin wanted that sketch. He'd ask; I'd say no way. He'd plead; I'd promised to keep the drawings a secret. Then Jimmy got sick and it didn't look like he'd finish his car. Ted kept after me and when that didn't work, he lied.

"Jimmy's in the hospital and he's not gonna get to race. He wants you to show me his car design." Reluctantly, I agreed.

Jimmy got better, just in time for the race. When his dad pushed the bright blue derby car to the top of the hill, Ted pushed his car, painted with the same design, along side. Jimmy was furious. So mad, in fact, that he wouldn't talk to me. And after the race, Jimmy and his dad loaded the car into their truck and sped off. They moved the next week. I never had a chance to explain.

Years later, I helped my boys with their Pinewood Derby cars. Memories of the Soap Box Derby resonated. My boys couldn't ride in their cars, but their Pinewood cars could wear a winning design. In the far starting block was an older, yet familiar face. The man lifted his son onto the platform for the start of the race—in his hand, a navy blue car, with white flames.

James.

I reached into my pocket and pulled out the drawing I'd held onto since sixth grade. Catching Jim's attention, I held up the sketch. The man worked his way toward me then wrapped his arms around me. "You were the best friend I ever had in elementary school. I'm sorry I acted like that." Now we're grade-school friends all over again.

Our stubbornness often deprives us of a second chance for forgiveness. Samson's anger and hurt was so intense that, for a while, he walked away from the woman he loved. When he cooled off and went back for her, she was gone and in the arms of another man.

I'm sure God occasionally gets miffed with me, but He never walks away. He promises that He'll always stand by us, even when we turn our backs on Him.

Has someone hurt you, betrayed your trust? Have you walked away in anger? Turn around and run back before it's too late.

Prayer

Lord, lead me to always show forgiveness.

BUILDING BLOCKS OF FAITH

Anger, left unchecked, will steal away what is valuable.

He Said, *She Said*

Journal

In Sickness & Wealth
He Said

When he heard this, Jesus said, "This sickness will not end in death. No, it is for God's glory so that God's Son may be glorified through it." Jesus loved Martha and her sister and Lazarus. Yet when he heard that Lazarus was sick, he stayed where he was two more days.

John 11:4-6 (NIV)

"Back so soon?" my wife said.

"Was hungry. What's for dinner?"

"Did you drop the key off like I asked?"

I ripped open a bag of chips. "Put it under the pot, just like you said."

"And the prayer shawl?"

"Hung it on the latch. You started supper, yet?"

"Hold it. You hung what on the latch?"

"The prayer shawl."

"You took it out of the package? Why?"

"Package? Never saw any package. Just the white shawl on the passenger seat"

"That was my scarf! Don't tell me you gave Ernie my

scarf!"

"Ok, I won't."

"How could you be so stupid?"

"Lots of practice," I said. "What's for supper?"

"Whatever you pick up for yourself on your way back from getting my scarf."

A few minutes later, I delivered Ernie's prayer shawl and retrieved my wife's scarf, but the ordeal got me to thinking about how we should pray for those who are sick. After all, I'd mistakenly delivered the wrong stole. What if my prayers were wrong, too?

When Jesus heard Lazarus was sick, He delayed. Why, I don't know. Jesus loved Lazarus. Loved him so much that he wept at the news of his death. So why wait? Why let him die? Why let any of us die?

Christ took His time. His time. Perhaps that's the point of the passage. Our time is borrowed, a gift on loan from God. But it's never really ours.

"This sickness will not end in death," Christ said. But it did. And then it didn't. Lazarus rose, walked, and lived again.

What do we make of life when the dead don't stay dead? How do we relate to a God who seems to ignore our prayers? Where do we turn when we have no hope? Perhaps the answer lies in the knowledge that God is good, great, and sometimes slow, but never late.

Not even when we think He is.

Prayer

Lord, may I see your hand at work through the suffering and remember: The sting of death is but a pinch for those in Christ.

BUILDING BLOCKS OF FAITH

God is good, God is great. God is slow, but never late.

He Said, *She Said*

Journal

....
....
....
....
....
....
....
....
....
....
....
....
....
....
....
....
....
....
....
....
....
....
....
....
....
....
....
....
....
....

In Joy & Borrow

She Said

When he heard this, Jesus said, "This sickness will not end in death. No, it is for God's glory so that God's Son may be glorified through it." Jesus loved Martha and her sister and Lazarus. Yet when he heard that Lazarus was sick, he stayed where he was two more days.

John 11:4-6 NIV

Suction cups, I wondered?

My son pressed the button in the elevator and the doors opened. "Mom, stop worrying. Sometimes Jesus has suction cups on His feet. That's what makes Him walk so slow!"

I smiled at the mental picture my son offered. We'd gone through a series of tests to measure my oldest son's intelligence. Now we waited. I was ready for it to be over. I was ready for the final verdict. If we just had the answer, we could move on with our lives. But a few minutes later, we exited the geneticist's office with an appointment for yet another round of tests.

I wondered what was taking God so long.

I'm sure Mary and Martha wondered, too. When Christ

heard that his friend Lazarus was sick, he delayed coming. It was if Jesus wanted his friend to die. And yet, I admit. I've felt that way at times, too. When I saw the suffering of my father, the way he coughed, the sunken sockets of his eyes, the pallor of his skin and the way it pressed against the cheekbones of his face, I said, "Oh Lord, just take him. Relieve the suffering."

But He didn't. Dad lived on. Hanging around. Wasting away. What was the glory in that?

After our final round of tests I learned my son carried a broken X chromosome—the marker for mental retardation. Did my waiting, my impatience help or hurt the process? Would it have prevented Chase's handicap if they'd diagnosed the problem sooner? Where was the glory in that?

Chase was born broken. As Lazarus was. As I am. As we all are.

Could it be that Christ didn't rush to save Lazarus because his friend was in no danger of dying? At least, not in the final way we think of death? Now we're talking real glory.

Regardless of my son's condition, I love him anyway. Perhaps I love him more because of it. His brokenness reveals God's grace, for there is not a purer heart than Chases'. When God's power meets our weakness, His glory shines.

Pray for healing? Yes. Hate the disease? Yes. Comfort, care and sit with those you love? Absolutely. Then wait on God. Even when He's slow to answer (walking with suction cups on His feet), the glory is there. Through our trust, He is glorified and we are saved.

Prayer

Father, bear with me while I learn to wait.

BUILDING BLOCKS OF FAITH

The timing of God is divine.

Journal

....
....
....
....
....
....
....
....
....
....
....
....
....
....
....
....
....
....
....
....
....
....
....
....
....
....
....
....
....
....
....
....

Diapers, Daycare & Diplomas

Prodigal Dad

He Said

The younger one said to his father, "Father, give me my share of the estate."...[And] he set off for a distant country and there squandered his wealth in wild living.

Luke 15:12-23 NIV

As a dad, it's hard to let go when your boy heads off in the wrong direction. I know. My son is heading down the wrong path.

I'm a graduate of State University. My father-in-law graduated from State, too. Our oldest son will graduate from State next year and we had a cousin who graduated from State not long ago. We've never had a family member graduate from that *other* university, although I did have an uncle on my dad's side that studied there for one semester before leaving to fight the Germans. The point is that the men in our family do not squander their family's educational dollars on wild living and low education at the university of baby blue, but that's exactly what my youngest wants to do.

And I support him. Not because I think it's the right

route. From my perspective, that other university is the path to perdition. But I support my boy's right to find his own way in this world, even if it hurts both of us.

As a son, I'm haunted by the fear that my father never approved of me. Dad's dead now, but he told me before he left that he was proud of me. It was a bedside confession and he might have been trying to settle accounts, but I believe he meant it. Still, it would have been nice to hear it sooner, like during my rebellious years when I was tearing up his tools and car and dishonoring his name.

The Prodigal Father loved his son despite the boy's shameful actions. He loved, gave and then watched as his son left for a world of sin and when he could do no more, he simply prayed. A dad like that is a big man, the kind of father I'd like to become someday.

If you're a dad or mom and worried that your son or daughter might embarrass you by their choice of schools, career or clothes, remember that the Prodigal Father received back more than a son when he let go. He got back a man and a lifetime of love.

Love your children. Let them go. Leave them in the care of God. Trust that our Father will show them the right path. God is a much better scout than we could ever be.

Prayer

Father, help me to love, let go and look to you for the protection of my children.

BUILDING BLOCKS OF FAITH

Some are called to greatness and some are called to serve. I'm called "Dad" and that's fine with me.

He Said, *She Said*

Journal

....
....
....
....
....
....
....
....
....
....
....
....
....
....
....
....
....
....
....
....
....
....
....
....
....
....
....
....
....
....

Radical Mom

She Said

The younger one said to his father, "Father, give me my share of the estate."...[And] he set off for a distant country and there squandered his wealth in wild living.

Luke 15:12-23 *NIV*

I watched as a sparrow swooped in and out of the birdhouse, its movements quick and determined. There was a sense of urgency in its flight. The bird darted back and forth, carrying twigs, leaves and grass into the box. After a time the sparrow poked her head from the box, exasperated. I imagined her peeps yelling, "Mom, feed me. Mom, he's touching me. Mom, make him stop."

As a mother of four boys, my head spins as I try to keep my flock together. Just making sure they get to the car without breaking into a brawl is a major task. When I'm shoving them out the door with a milk jug in one hand, bag lunch clinched between my teeth, and a container of fruit under my arm, my head seems to explode. And still, in spite of the chaos, I've never

113

regretted one moment with my boys. Not even when they needed the radical radiation of tough love.

I've always said if one of our boys strayed, I'd never turn away. I'd do what I could to bring him back. But when he stole five thousand dollars from his brother, ran from the law, and rejected our help, I was forced to love him from afar—to watch as the consequences of his actions crushed him. I saw him flounder, fall and blame others, until finally he returned home. When at last he collapsed into my arms, his mistakes seemed minor. He was my son. He was home.

Sometimes our parental love is stretched beyond the breaking point. It is then, when we think we'll snap, that we must hold on tight. It is the defining moment when we choose our child over our own pride and pain. When we cling to the frayed edges of a relationship, there is still hope that we can save them, bring them back to us and to God.

Have you felt the bonds of love breaking? Hang on. Hold tight. Hope always. You're child's future may depend on it.

Prayer

Lord, I am so glad You welcome me home when I wander away.

Help me to come back and run to the ones I love.

BUILDING BLOCKS OF FAITH

You cannot hug with crossed arms.

He Said, *She Said*

Journal

....
....
....
....
....
....
....
....
....
....
....
....
....
....
....
....
....
....
....
....
....
....
....
....
....
....
....
....
....
....

Dissing Dad

He Said

*Honor your father and your mother, so that you may live
long in the land the LORD your God is giving you.*

Exodus 20:12 *NIV*

Fathers used to hold a place of honor in the home, but no
more. Today, fathers are portrayed as stupid, insensitive and lazy.
A recent television ad showed a computer-illiterate father trying
to help his daughter with homework. The daughter, with a look
of irritation on her face, turns to her mother for help who then
dismisses the father, sending him outside to wash the dog.

It wasn't always this way.

Before Herman Munster, Archie Bunker and Homer
Simpson there was Andy Taylor, Ward Clever and Father
Knows Best. Dads served as the head of the household, earned
the majority of the income and provided wise council. We
represented on earth the goodness, protection and wisdom of
our heavenly Father.

But we have turned God into our buddy and sent dads
to the entertainment room. For over half a century, we have

acted as if dads don't matter. The result is rampant promiscuity, single-moms and deadbeat dads. We have two income families that can't make ends meet and homes shuttered from broken marriages.

We have to restore fathers as the central figure in the home and men it begins with us.

It is time we reassert our role as head of the home and resist the cultural forces that would make us irrelevant. We must insist upon respect, even when we fail, because God has placed us in a position of leadership. The family is His concept, not ours, and the burden of leadership is great.

But we cannot treat wives as lesser partners. They are not. They are created in the image of God and deserve both our respect and love. This too is God's will. If you think she is your trophy, you don't deserve her. If you think she is your maid, you are mistaken. If you think she is your wench, you are wrong.

Women, love your husband. Honor, respect and call him to account. This is the language we understand. But if we fail to live up to your expectations,, do not treat us with disgust. Instead, pray for us. Who knows how many sins you may cover with your mercy, love and tender grace?

Prayer

O God, Holy is your name. Help me to honor the title of
"Father" by being the dad you called me to be.

BUILDING BLOCKS OF FAITH

If you demand respect and recognition, chances are you aren't

worthy of the applause.

He Said, *She Said*

Journal

....
....
....
....
....
....
....
....
....
....
....
....
....
....
....
....
....
....
....
....
....
....
....
....
....
....
....
....
....
....
....
....

Dismissing Mom

She Said

*Honor your father and your mother, so that you may live
long in the land the LORD your God is giving you.*

Exodus 20:12

The line at the store was long—one register with ten folks
waiting to be served. Thank goodness I was at the front. A woman
stood behind me, her four-year-old daughter lay screaming in the
buggy, "I want crayons!"

When her mother reached to lift the little girl, her daughter
smacked her in the mouth three times, drawing blood with the
last lick.

It wasn't my place nor my business, but as the child drew
back a fourth time I snagged her hand in mid-air.

"Hey!" I said, "That's your mother." I gently twisted her
toward me and pointed my finger, "You're way too little to be
slapping such a beautiful mom." Stunned, the child hushed.

Her mother stared. "She mimics her father."

"Then her mother should get help." I handed her a tissue
to blot the blood.

As a society, we've failed our families. Men slap their wives for sport, women trade their self-respect for soiled affection, and our teens run wild in the streets. Our homes are in shambles. It is time we, as Christians women, reclaimed the mantel of housewife and homemaker.

Parenting is a gift, but the responsibility is great, and we have failed our children. When parents cut, criticize and belittle each other, we hurt not just each other, but our children, too. How can a son or daughter learn respect for their parents if mom and dad dismiss one another with sarcasm and ridicule? Not all abuse is physical. In fact, the wounds of verbal abuse linger within the heart of a broken soul.

God holds parents in the highest regard. He calls our offspring "a blessing." Today's children are tomorrow's parents. Do you honor yours? When the phone rings and you check the caller ID, do you dismiss your mom's call as an unwelcome intrusion? Remember, your children are learning from your example.

Honor your father and mother. Show respect. Demonstrate love. In the end, we will reap what we sow.

Prayer

Lord, cradle me in your arms when I feel neglected, forgotten and humiliated.

BUILDING BLOCKS OF FAITH

God didn't invented Mother's Day, but he invented mothers.

Remember yours daily.

He Said, She Said

Journal

....
....
....
....
....
....
....
....
....
....
....
....
....
....
....
....
....
....
....
....
....
....
....
....
....
....
....
....
....
....
....

Throw 'em Out
He Said

"Your children hasten back,...Lift up your eyes and look around; all your children gather and come to you. As surely as I live," declares the LORD, "you will wear them all as ornaments; you will put them on, like a bride."

Isaiah 49:17-18 NIV

We started a new tradition this Christmas that I hope never to repeat. It's called, "Where's Mason?"

My youngest asked if he could work in the Keys over his winter break. We wanted him home. He needed the money. His college debt won out.

He arrived in Florida a week before Christmas just ahead of rain, a cold front and a management shake up that left him bussing tables instead of taking tips. Here would be the perfect place to compare my son's quest to that of the prodigal boy who squandered his dad's inheritance, but I won't.

Oh, okay, maybe I will just a little.

Both boys left home and journeyed to a far away country. (The unofficial motto of Key West is, "Welcome to The Conch

Republic. We seceded where others failed.") Both fell in with a fast crowd. (You ever driven in South Florida? Scary.) Both ended up working in less than desirable jobs. (One fed pigs. The other had to endure boorish behavior.) You get the picture.

My son called Christmas Eve to say he'd made a mistake. He wanted to come home. Being the wise, loving, and understanding dad that I am, I told him, "Too bad! You're the one who wanted to go down there. You're the one who broke your mom's heart, ditched Ralphie, skipped out on the Griswolds' Christmas Vacation, shunned the reading of the *Polar Express* and ruined Christmas morning, day and dinner for everyone. This was all your idea. Deal with it."

Just kidding. I didn't really say all that. I would have, but my wife yanked the phone away. She's better at expressing the spirit of Christmas than I am. And what is the spirit of Christmas? It's forgiveness, compassion, kindness, humility, gentleness, and patience. The sort of attributes I should model, but don't.

I missed Mason this Christmas and take comfort in the promise that he'll return home. But he's also hanging out with us on the tree this year.

Each day I pause to look at his ornaments. A soccer ball with his name on it. A hand made craft project with his face glued to the front. Sailing reminders and snowboard figurines, school emblems and Popsicle sticks shaped like a reindeer. "You will wear them all as ornaments," Isaiah promised.

I'm glad Mason's safe, thankful that he's motivated to work. But I'm also mindful of the other sons, husbands and fathers who aren't working in the Keys this Christmas, but are stationed, instead, on the front lines, risking their lives that my family might remain safe this Christmas. "Lift up your eyes and look around; all your children gather."

I pray it will be so. Hurry home, Son. We miss you.

Prayer

Father, do you miss me the way I miss my boys? If so, call.

BUILDING BLOCKS OF FAITH

To father a child is easy. It's growing into the title that consumes your life and makes you worthy of the name.

He Said, *She Said*

Journal

....
....
....
....
....
....
....
....
....
....
....
....
....
....
....
....
....
....
....
....
....
....
....
....
....
....
....
....
....
....
....
....

Dust 'em Off

She Said

"Your children hasten back,...Lift up your eyes and look around; all your children gather and come to you. As surely as I live," declares the LORD, "you will wear them all as ornaments; you will put them on, like a bride."

Isaiah 49:17-18 NIV

Sometimes we do for the good of the many at the cost of the one—even when the decision crushes our hearts.

My husband tightened the last screw into the lock. "This is our home. We shouldn't have to put locks on our door." He dropped the screwdriver in his toolbox and walked into our son's room.

"Box up his stuff. All of it. He's got to hit bottom before he'll change."

That night every item I packed away was bathed in tears. Our child—lost. We had to push him away, turn our backs for a time and pray that God would restore him.

Five years passed—two without any word, any news, any

knowledge. The rest, sporadic sightings of him from a distance. Shoving him away was the hardest thing we'd ever done; the sacrifice of the one for health and safety for the rest of our family.

God moved away from His children for a time, too. They had to hit bottom in order to be restored. Renovation isn't a pretty process. Walls are ripped down, wires uncrossed, foundations repaired. But God promised to refurbish, build up and repair. He promised to bring our children, and His, back. To gather them around us.

I prayed every morning this year that God would restore my family. Bring our prodigal home to the arms of the parents who love him. As Christmas approached, we heard he was on his way. But we'd heard this before and he was always a no-show. Would he "no-show" again?

Christmas arrived. Our door opened and there was our prodigal. Home. I gazed across the room at our four sons laughing together as though no time had passed. Not only had God restored our family, but He'd wiped away the hurt of memories past. Our home was filled with joy and when the evening ended, I took a picture of our boys, gathered together, and placed it near my heart. "You will wear them all as ornaments."

God is a God of restoration. He understands tough love and the pain it demands. But He delights in healing.

Have you felt the sting of loss? What treasured relationship needs to be restored in the New Year? Let the Master Carpenter do His job.

Prayer

Precious Lord, keep our children safe beneath Your wings.

BUILDING BLOCKS OF FAITH

Love always demands a price and Jesus is our receipt.

He Said, *She Said*
Journal

....
....
....
....
....
....
....
....
....
....
....
....
....
....
....
....
....
....
....
....
....
....
....
....
....
....
....
....
....
....
....
....
....

G.I. Joe

He Said

*An angel of the Lord appeared to him in a dream and said,
"Joseph son of David, do not be afraid to take Mary home
as your wife, because what is conceived in her is
from the Holy Spirit."*

Matthew 1:20 NIV

"What I want for Christmas is..."

When I was a boy, the Sears catalog sat on the corner of the hearth in our den with dog-eared pages and pictures circled in red ink. At least once each Christmas, my dad would say, "Son, you already have a G. I. Joe. Several, in fact."

"Yeah, but not enough for a platoon."

The soldiers from the Sears "Wish Book" became my make-believe comrades. I'd dress them out, arrange their weapons and bring them to life...and death. G. I. Joe was a soldier, after all, a warrior in waiting.

When God dreamed of Christmas morning, He sought a warrior in waiting, too—an action figure that would survive the battle.

133

God's Joe, like my Joes, came alive in dreams and visions. He advanced on the news of the heavenly herald, took courage in the command to be brave, reaffirmed his commitment to Mary and accepted his mission without wavering. In the same way, my G. I. Joe brought joy to me Christmas morning, Joseph, son of David, brought a smile to God when he said "yes" to the call. God still calls. He calls us to large, life-changing moments that challenge our character, defy our plans and break the action-figure persona we present to others.

Joseph went to bed a fiancée. He awoke destined to become a step-father to a son born in wedlock, but not of his flock. His call to action was a blessing and burden, a dream and nightmare. That's the trouble with warriors in waiting. They become wounded.

What dream has God placed in your heart? What Christmas morning wish remains buried under the fear of saying "yes" to God? Do not disregard the impact of a "Wish Book" action figure. It may be God is calling you to come alive.

Prayer

Lord, you are the giver of dreams. Give me more than I can unwrap.

BUILDING BLOCKS OF FAITH

You can give without loving, but you can't love without giving.

He Said, *She Said*
Journal

....
....
....
....
....
....
....
....
....
....
....
....
....
....
....
....
....
....
....
....
....
....
....
....
....
....
....
....
....
....
....
....

Sometimes just showing up for the passage is a gift of love.

"Oh! My God"

She Said

*An angel of the Lord appeared to him in a dream and said,
"Joseph son of David, do not be afraid to take Mary home
as your wife, because what is conceived in her is
from the Holy Spirit."*

Matthew 1:2 NIV

I stared at the shelf below the bathroom mirror. The night light cast a yellow haze through the room, illuminating the outline of the tiny vial, the image unclear. Just flipping on the overhead light twisted a knot in my stomach.

In those days, pregnancy tests were new and pricey. Today, they're purchased in packs for under twenty bucks, with results that appear instantaneously. I had to wait 4-6 hours. Reading the test wasn't easy either. Inside the tube, a solid deposit of sediment meant sadness—a solid center with a dark ring, joy. I turned on the light and squinted. Joy!

Joseph and Mary, on the other hand, had the surprise of

their lives. There was no early pregnancy test to prepare them. I could only imagine Mary's response, much less that of Joseph.

"Oh! My God!" Joseph might have said.

"Indeed, He is." Replied the angel.

Talk about faith! They had it. The culture alone would shun the fathers and serve the women a death sentence for a child conceived out of wedlock. God had chosen this time for Christ's birth, knowing the hardships a pregnancy would bring before marriage. He could have waited until the couple married. There would have been no questions, but that would have lessened the miracle. The gift of Christ had to come through two individuals who could withstand the blessings and the trials. This child had to come as a miracle and He had to be accepted and loved unconditionally by the parents God had chosen.

There was more to the birth of Christ than just a miraculous conception. It was about faith. Joseph trusted and obeyed the angel's instructions. He believed the woman he loved had not betrayed him, and he took action to protect her and the child entrusted to his care. Christ's entire beginning was based on absolute faith and trust, the groundwork for the ministry that changed the world and saved our souls.

My pregnancy ended three weeks later, but Mary saw hers to the conclusion. His birth, His death, and His resurrection happened because of the faith of one man and one woman chosen for the work.

Joseph and Mary weren't preachers. They were willing servants—everyday folks with regular lives who obeyed when God called. Are you willing to serve? What has God called you to do?

It could be a miracle.

Prayer

Father, may we be willing servants.

BUILDING BLOCKS OF FAITH

"Lord, I'll take two servings of sacrifice, with a side order of giving, please."

He Said, She Said

Journal

....
....
....
....
....
....
....
....
....
....
....
....
....
....
....
....
....
....
....
....
....
....
....
....
....
....
....
....
....
....
....
....

Joseph Stepped Up
He Said

And there were shepherds living out in the fields nearby,
keeping watch over their flocks at night. An angel of the
Lord appeared to them, and the glory of the Lord shone
around them, and they were terrified. But the angel said to
them, "Do not be afraid."

Luke 2:10-12 NIV

Joseph missed out on the honeymoon. Presidents get them. Newlyweds, too. Even coaches, clergy and couches get a period of adjustment. Not Joseph. He missed out on his honeymoon. All he got was a pregnant virgin, which is way different than getting a virgin pregnant.

Mary was young, Joseph just old. Stable, but seasoned and set in his ways. Still, Joe was a reverent man, so when God's angel told Joe to take a three day trek with his pregnant fiancée, Joe obeyed, enduring the shame and scorn of the pedestrians pointing from the roadside. The unwed couple's sin was evident for all to see.

I'm glad Joe was Jesus' step-dad. A lot of men wouldn't have put up with the humiliation. I'd have claimed my rights, threatened to sue my ex future in-laws and gone on talk TV to let the world know that I'd never touched her, that the child wasn't mine.

But not Joe. He honored his bride-to-be by doing what was right by her and ordained by God.

Yes, Joseph should have called ahead, planned better and left sooner. He should have tried harder to find his fiancée a birthing room on this, the most important night of her life. But in the end he did what he could. He stepped up, took responsibility for her safety and stood by her.

A lot of single moms could use a good Joe. They need a husband who'll stay, work and sacrifice for the children in her home, even if they aren't his. God knew what He was doing when He picked Joe to be the earthly father figure in Christ's life. He knew what He was doing when He made you a dad, too.

If you're a father who doesn't know where his children are,

it's time you stepped up.

Prayer

Lord, I'm a man created in your image. When the role of father becomes difficult, help me get up, step up and shut up.

BUILDING BLOCKS OF FAITH

In God's eyes, we're all a success waiting to happen. We just need to take that first step and respond to God's call.

He Said, She Said
Journal

....
....
....
....
....
....
....
....
....
....
....
....
....
....
....
....
....
....
....
....
....
....
....
....
....
....
....
....
....
....
....

He Should've Called Ahead

She Said

And there were shepherds living out in the fields nearby, keeping watch over their flocks at night. An angel of the Lord appeared to them, and the glory of the Lord shone around them, and they were terrified. But the angel said to them, "Do not be afraid."

Luke 2:10-12 NIV

Mary rubbed her back and tried to reposition herself on the donkey. "That's the fifth inn we've stopped at. They can't all be full."

"There's another around the corner," said Joseph, leading them down a dark alley.

"You should've told your family we were coming."

"You want that I should let my brother see you like this, God forbid?"

144

"Oh, so now all this is *my* fault, now?"

"Well, *I'm* not to blame."

"You should've planned better, Joe. Did you think this baby would wait?"

"Who could have known there would be such a crowd?"

"It's a census, you idiot! Look, there's the last inn. As long as you're checking, see if the honeymoon suite is available. Better yet, ask about separate rooms."

Joe should have known better. There has never been room for God. Not in an inn, not in our hearts. The cares of the world crowd Him out.

But when Mary and Joseph arrived in Bethlehem, suddenly there was room for all. From the night he was born until the day He died, the Christ child drew a crowd. People flocked to hear him speak, teach and heal. There were days when the crowds were so large that He had to climb into a boat to keep from being crushed.

No, Joseph may not have called ahead and planned properly, but God did. He knew that as long as His Son strolled the streets and countryside, Jesus would be hard pressed to fit in, that few would welcome Him into their heart.

Do you have space for Christ? Have you made room for Him in your day? Does He have a seat at your table, by your bed and in your thoughts? Are you still keeping Christ in the stall out back while you warm yourself by the hearth? If so, maybe it's time the two of you swapped places.

Prayer

Lord, help me to step up and be the man you called me to be
for my wife, children and parents.

BUILDING BLOCKS OF FAITH

A goat can father a kid but only a dad can rear a child.

He Said, *She Said*
Journal

....
....
....
....
....
....
....
....
....
....
....
....
....
....
....
....
....
....
....
....
....
....
....
....
....
....
....
....
....
....
....
....
....
....

J.O.B.- JUST OVER BROKE:

LOVING YOUR WORK

Have Work Your Way At Bigger King

He Said

Praise the LORD, my soul, and forget not all his benefits, who forgives all your sins and heals all your diseases, who redeems your life from the pit and crowns you with love and compassion, who satisfies your desires with good things so that your youth is renewed like the eagle's.

Psalm 103:2-6 NIV

In these tough economic times when companies are downsizing, outsourcing and capsizing, it's hard to find the perfect job and, by "perfect job," I mean any job that comes with benefits...like a paycheck. That's why I suggest you apply to Bigger King, whose motto is: Have Work Your Way.

I know what you're thinking. You're thinking, "Great, another start-up company that's gonna go under after three months." Trust me, Bigger King isn't going anywhere but up. They've been servicing customers for centuries. Here are a few reasons you should consider going to work for Bigger King.

He Said, She Said

He forgives all your sins: If you mess up, don't worry. Our boss at Bigger King isn't a screamer. He expects perfection, but gives you plenty of time to grow into the job. We had this one employee, Paul, who, no matter how hard he tried, couldn't do the right thing. Even said as much in his letters. The boss promoted him anyway. Moved him from a small territory in Asia to the regional office in Rome. This gives you some idea of what a great guy our boss is.

Heals all your diseases: We have a great medical plan at Bigger King. If you get sick or injured, don't worry. Our boss will take care of you. Even if you become deathly ill and can't work, he'll stay right by your bed, encouraging you to get better, reminding you that you're loved, missed, and that your work is important to him.

Redeems your life from the pit: If you think your last job was the pits, you'll love working here. You can do any work you want. Seriously. Even if you stink at it. Our boss provides all the training and education you'll need. He places a lot of emphasis on heart, so if you think you can, with him, you can.

Crowns you with love: The boss remembers your birthday, name, your kid's names, and anything that's important to you. Plus, if you need a hug, shoulder to cry on or ear to bend, he's there. His door is always open.

Crowns you with compassion: He knows how you feel and understands how hard life can be sometimes. Even though he owns the company, he once pretended to be a common laborer and took a job in his own company as a carpenter. Before long, he was right back at the top, leading, teaching and helping others. When the boss man says, "I know how you feel," he really knows you feel.

Satisfies your desires with good things: You don't have to "settle" for any old job. The boss man wants you to have a good job. That's part of Bigger King's mission statement. "I came to give you abundant life."

Your youth is renewed: We have a great fitness and wellness program. It's called work. No one gets laid off, takes a "package," or retires. Work with us and you'll die with a smile on your face doing what you love doing.

There you are. The basic package at Bigger King. Don't ask what it pays. Your needs will be covered. Ask instead, "where do I sign up?"

Prayer

Lord, satisfy my desire for fulfillment by putting me to work for You.

BUILDING BLOCKS OF FAITH

Working for the King has its perks.

He Said, *She Said*

Journal

....

....

....

....

....

....

....

....

....

....

....

....

....

....

....

....

....

....

....

....

....

....

....

....

....

....

....

....

....

....

....

....

I Forgot

She Said

Praise the LORD, O my soul, and forget not all his benefits- who forgives all your sins and heals all your diseases, who redeems your life from the pit and crowns you with love and compassion, who satisfies your desires with good things so that your youth is renewed like the eagle's.

Psalm 103:2-5 NIV

My son stood, hands clasping his cheeks, mouth open. He'd forgotten again. The kid was notorious for leaving something at home. One day it was homework, the next a book—always something.

We'd just pulled up to the front of the school when he realized he'd left his saxophone at home. He climbed out of the car and headed up the sidewalk, expecting me to run back home and bail him out... again. But no more. He'd forgotten for the last time. It was time he learned to remember the benefits of keeping up with things.

I forget a lot, too. I don't mean to, but I do. I forget the discernment God gives me when there are important decisions looming. I forget to say thanks for a friend who's health has been restored. I forget that I wouldn't be where I am today if God hadn't bailed me out of a bad marriage or helped me deal with my son's disability. I forget, too.

But God never forgets.

He remembers what is important and forgets the sins we confess. He wipes away the memory of my mistakes and loves me anyway. I don't deserve it, but He does. He's just that way.

I didn't go back to the house and my son received a failing grade because of his forgetfulness. But eventually he did learn the importance of remembering.

So have I. These days I don't just pray; I write my prayers because it prevents me from forgetting the benefits of His faithfulness and how immense His forgiveness is. It reminds me to praise Him continually for the vastness of His love.

It's never too early to forgive others and never too late to remember His goodness. When you start your day...remember His promises of protection. When the clock strikes noon... remember His promises of provision. When you crawl into bed... remember His promises of love.

And when you think of that person who's disappointed, offended or hurt you, forget it. As His children, we have more important things to remember.

He Said, *She Said*

Prayer

Oh Lord, You are merciful. Your grace is sufficient.

BUILDING BLOCKS OF FAITH

Forgiveness is never a mistake.

He Said, *She Said*

Journal

....
....
....
....
....
....
....
....
....
....
....
....
....
....
....
....
....
....
....
....
....
....
....
....
....
....
....
....
....
....

From Pit to Prominence
He Said

*So the warden put Joseph in charge of all those held in the
prison, and he was made responsible for all that
was done there.*

Genesis 39:22 NIV

In his thirties, he led an e-business technology team from
a start-up company to its public stock offering. They went big,
made a splash in the press and then went looking for a new and
younger manager.

Suddenly retired, he helped found a new business. The
job took him to Asia where he met with top executives in the
semi-conductor industry. Modeling the successful strategy of his
previous job, he positioned the firm to go public. But days before
their announcement, the global economy burped; investors
pulled back, the firm floundered. For two years, he watched as
one angel investor after another waltzed by his office, but none
came bearing good news and gifts. The firm folded.

In order to pay the bills, he began restoring homes, adding
decks, and refinishing rooms. Of course, business thrived. He

hired additional help, rebuilt his savings and discovered he enjoyed working with his hands, going to bed tired and waking up in better shape than the day before. He dropped pounds, added muscle, plus a few more clients. Over coffee one morning, a customer commented on his leadership skills. "Would you like to have a job with an office, benefits and stock options?" his friend asked.

"Only if it presents a challenge."

Soon his unit led the company in growth, profits and efficiency. He was tapped to head a new division. The promotion would double his salary and vastly increase his responsibility. Then, on the eve of the announcement, he was fired. He learned later his knowledge, experience and wisdom had posed a threat to the owner. But none of that mattered on his drive home from work. With his wife recently retired, a new set of grand babies due and a suspicious mass on his spine, life's circumstances dumped him in the pit, again.

Joseph suffered betrayal, mistreatment and misfortune, too. Told by God that he would become a grand leader, Joseph struggled with the mantle of greatness. "Listen to the dream I had," said Joseph. "I had another dream... No one is greater in this house than I am...When all goes well with you, remember me... show me kindness... mention me... I have done nothing to deserve being put in a pit." His arrogant attitude bred jealousy and resentment, leading others to forget and forsake him.

God has made each of us responsible for someone and something. Whether we're serving time in prison, serving soup to the homeless, or serving on the board of a fortune 500 company, our attitude toward others reflects our heart for God.

When my friend arrived home that final evening, he hugged his wife, held her hand and prayed for God to see them through the crisis—just as they'd done in times past. I have no doubt he'll rise, again, from pit to prominence. That's what men of God do.

If you feel imprisoned, don't despair. God's promises, power and protection will set you free if you will trust, work and wait upon Him.

Prayer

My Father, you are in heaven and I am here. You see me in the pit and at the pinnacle of my success. You are my God. I will serve no other.

BUILDING BLOCKS OF FAITH

The journey is never over until the anchor is set.

He Said, She Said
Journal

Down in the Hole

She Said

So the warden put Joseph in charge of all those held in the
prison, and he was made responsible for
all that was done there.

Genesis 39:22 NIV

The kennel door creaked as we pushed it open. A bouncy
Golden Retriever puppy straddled my knee then licked my
neck—happy to have someone pay attention. This was not a
responsibility I wanted. Neither did my veterinarian friend. But
we were saddled with the nasty task.

I wrapped my arms around the puppy and pressed his head
tight against my chest. He needed to know he was loved, even if it
was only for a few minutes. I kissed him between the ears.

"Don't drag this out. It's hard enough as it is."

"I know. I know."

Stilling the rambunctious pup, I wrapped my hand around
his foreleg and rolled the vein into view. The vet pulled the pink
liquid into the syringe. Slipping the needle into the vein, the
pup whined from the prick. He nodded for me to release my

grip. Relaxing my fingers, the fluid seeped into the vein. One, two, three beats and the lethal drug hit his heart. The pup licked my chin and grew limp in my arms. His heart stopped...his life snuffed out.

In my 15 years of work with a veterinarian, most was joyful. The work was hard and it wasn't all wagging tails and sloppy licks. There was this part too, and the dungeon we looked up from held hundreds of healthy animals sentenced to death because the shelter was overflowing.

Joseph spent his time in the hole as well. Tossed away by his brothers like a piece of trash, he was left to die at the hands of the enemy. He did his time, even caused some trouble and agony, but he did not go unrecognized by God. He was given charge and though he'd done some things he didn't want to do, he eventually made a difference.

At times, we're all thrown in the pits—each one suffering a private prison of some sort. Christ accepted the position of Savior knowing His prison would be filled with souls just like mine...souls who needed to be saved and He was willing to feel the prick of death for us. Straight from the right hand of God, He lowered Himself into the pits without hesitation with the intention of saving me.

The daunting task of euthanasia was one of the darkest places I've been. I hated it and though I was able to save a few mommas and their babies, it wasn't enough. Just as I longed to save the puppies, Jesus longs to save us.

Sometimes, like Joseph, we're taken from the pit and located in a place of prominence. Other times, like Jesus, we're taken from prominence into the pit. Either way, it's what we do with the charge we've been given. Joseph changed lives...Jesus changed the world.

If you're in a hole and life looks impossible, if the needle of death is pricking your heart, let Christ take hold. He will free you from the prison that holds you. Won't you let Him?

Prayer

Father, look down on me and pull me from the pit.

BUILDING BLOCKS OF FAITH

Look closely at those around you. Show kindness. You may save someone from the pit.

He Said, She Said

Journal

....
....
....
....
....
....
....
....
....
....
....
....
....
....
....
....
....
....
....
....
....
....
....
....
....
....
....
....
....
....
....

Take a Chance... Advance!

He Said

*Don't waste your time on useless work, mere busywork,
the barren pursuits of darkness. Expose these things for the
sham they are. It's a scandal when people waste their lives
on things they must do in the darkness where no one will
see. Rip the cover off those frauds and see how   attractive they look in the light of Christ. Wake up from your
sleep, Climb out of your coffins; Christ will show you the
light! So watch your step. Use your head. Make the most of
every chance you get. These are desperate times!*

Ephesians 5:11-16 (The Message)

When did "work" become a four-letter word? When did
God's first command become a burden? Perhaps it began when
we exchanged God's gift of enjoyment through employment for
the fleeting security of career entitlement. As the resource officer
waits for us to clear out our desk, we cry, "You can't do this
to me! I've been here since..." Work was meant for more than

165

provision, position and posturing. When we labor "heartily as unto the Lord," it becomes an act of worship.

I'm writing from the mountains today. We're preparing for our second Writer's Advance Event. I've attended other writer's retreats, but the idea of giving ground and falling back doesn't fit our calling. So, over the next few days, we'll discuss, prepare and advance toward the next big thing God has planned. There's snow on the ground, ice on the parking lot and fire in our bones.

How about you? Are you burned-out instead of on fire for a cause, craft or ministry? Do you fear you've missed your chance to "make" a difference? Don't worry. Our God is the Lord of second and third chances. His eyes roam the earth seeking those who will open the door when He knocks. Will you respond to his banging?

Here are four tips for how you can "make the most of every chance you get."

Find a problem and fix it. Opportunities are often disguised as problems. These challenges force us to explore other options, examine the resources we have, and push on. When faced with a dead end, listen for God to say, "This way." A closed door is only a dead end when you don't follow the detour signs.

Move with urgency. Open doors do not remain open forever. New opportunities are time-sensitive. Ground floors become foundations for tall buildings, so seize the moment. Don't wait, ponder, pray and procrastinate. By the time you act, it may be too late. If the chance to do something different, untried and frightening excites you, then step through the open door.

Expect resistance. Often we mistake hardships for God's disapproval when, in fact, the rocks, weeds and ruts are just confirmation that we're plowing new territory. The Apostle Paul wrote to the Church in Corinth, "A great and effective door has opened to me and there are many adversaries." The fastest point of sail is when the wind is against and slightly ahead of the boat, not blowing from behind. The gusts buffeting your cheeks could be God's breath cooling you down and keeping you refreshed.

Face down your fears. Don't let your fear of the unknown stop you from doing the thing that excites you. Wake up. Climb out. Watch your step. Use your head. Make the most of every chance you get. Christ will show you the light.

These are desperate times. The world needs pioneers who are willing to put aside the slothful acts of darkness and step boldly into the future. Today, if you feel God calling you to a new challenge, don't hesitate. Advance!

Prayer

Father, these are desperate times. We need pioneers with your vision. Inspire us!

BUILDING BLOCKS OF FAITH

Every valley has two mountains, so avoid looking back at your disappointments and look up instead, because that's where you'll find the next mountaintop experience." — *Unknown*

He Said, She Said
Journal

Wake Up!

She Said

Don't waste your time on useless work, mere busywork, the barren pursuits of darkness. Expose these things for the sham they are. It's a scandal when people waste their lives on things they must do in the darkness where no one will see. Rip the cover off those frauds and see how attractive they look in the light of Christ. Wake up from your sleep, Climb out of your coffins; Christ will show you the light! So watch your step. Use your head. Make the most of every chance you get. These are desperate times!

Ephesians 5:11-16 (The Message)

He shocked me. "Religion sucks." Tattooed from head to toe, his appearance sent a jolt of fear through me. But the more I learned of his story, the more inclined I was to agree.

Abused from childhood by his mother, abandoned by his father and shunned by his friends, this child grew into a man who believed in nothing, no one and no wonder. Even members of his church, the ones who really knew his family history, closed their eyes to his needs, choosing instead to call him a pagan and worse.

An elderly woman checked on him, from time to time. Slipped him some food, prayed for him. Thirty years later, he couldn't recall her name, so he just called her a Christian—the only one he'd ever known.

His shocking appearance and brazen judgment on the church was a wake up call for me. Had I overlooked him, too? In my sincere efforts to serve Christ, had I become so busy with the "goodness" of church that I'd shut my eyes to this man? Was it my fault he became the beast he was? Would a little love have cost that much?

Christ took time for me. He found time for people, not projects. Constantly in demand to teach, heal and feed, He was never too busy to stop and see the real hurt in a person, never too important to see their soul, never too good to humble Himself as a servant.

We see what we want to see, so we focus on the sins of others and not the grace of God. Condemn someone long enough and they'll think they're worthless. Correct and forgive and they'll know love. These are desperate times but we can't slow the pace of our planet. We can, however, touch the hearts of desperate people.

Wake up! Get up! Act like Christ. Don't waste your time on useless work. Waste it instead, on hopeless people.

Prayer

Lord, forgive me when I judge your children.

BUILDING BLOCKS OF FAITH

Assist, don't resist. Help, don't hinder. Seek...you will find.

He Said, She Said

Journal

Passing Grades
He Said

For all have sinned and fall short of the glory of God.
Romans 3:23 NIV

George broke his ankle last Saturday. He went to get his neighbor's paper, slipped on the ice in the driveway, got up, took a few more steps and fell again, snapping a bone. George can be hardheaded. Kind hearted, but hardheaded.

My aunt broke her hip during the same snowstorm. When my mom called to give me the news, I thought she said my aunt "fell off a sled." I never thought of my aunt as being old, even though she did need a hand crank to start her first car. Still, it seemed odd that my aunt, a grandmother of two on Medicare, would be out sledding in the snow. Turns out she fell off a "bed."

(Mom called on a cell phone which, as you know, is a portable electronic device used for taking pictures, sending pictures, surfing the web, playing video games, sending email, reading books, and listening to music. Occasionally people will also try to talk to other people with a cell phone, which my mom did, but I generally prefer that you write me a letter, since it's cheaper, faster and easier to understand.)

The same day George and my aunt fell, my friend, Cindy, fell—not in the snow, but to her knees. Here's a portion of the prayer she sent me.

"Lord, forgive me when I fail you. I pray so hard, but is it not enough? Is it wrong? Lord, I don't want to disappoint you, yet I know at times I do. So I pray that you will forgive me when I fail."

I wanted to push her down in the snow. "How can you fail God?" I asked. "He's God and we're just itty-bitty beings. We can fall, sure, but fail? Never."

If Christ is your teacher, then failure is not a possibility, though we may feel that way because the "Accuser of the Brethren" stands ready to bring false charges against us. He wants to weaken our resolve and beat us down. The Father of Lies is our prosecutor, charging us with violations of God's law, demanding that we be punished.

But God's grace delivers not retribution, but redemption. How can you fail God when His Son has taken the test for you?

Yes, we all fall short of the glory of God and, thank God we do. Otherwise, we might think we deserve the passing marks. But we don't. Christ does. And God bless Him, He never fails.

Prayer

Lord, I know of your great deeds. Help me to know your ways.

BUILDING BLOCKS OF FAITH

Trust God, not His methods.

He Said, *She Said*
Journal

Landing in "Grace"-land

She Said

For all have sinned and fall short of the glory of God.

Romans 3:23 NIV

One, two, three, four, five, six...I count the steps in my head every time I start down them. I started counting steps when the kids were little, after our son took a tumble.

Cameron was six when he fell. He stood at the top of the stairs in his Under-roos and matching Scooby-Doo socks, smiling and laughing. Tim stood behind him and I was at the bottom. I sat my load of laundry on the floor and turned just in time to see Cameron's feet slip. Horror stricken, Tim grabbed at him trying to grasp any part of his tumbling body. I did too, but missed. Cameron flipped twice, somersaulted down the stairs until he hit the wall, smacking his head against the railing.

Unconscious, we scooped him up and rushed him to the ER. The doctor examined him and sent him for x-rays. "You say he fell down the stairs?"

"Missed a step and his feet just flew out from under him. I tried to grab him, but was too late."

"Well, we'll keep your boy overnight until the swelling goes down, but I think he'll be fine."

I miss steps, too, and when I do I feel as though I've disappointed God. It seems the harder I try to be what God wants me to be, the more I trip and stumble—the more I feel I've let God down. My friend scolded me yesterday, told me there was no way I could let God down.

"You can't disappoint Him. He loves you too much. It's like saying your disabled son disappoints you—it just can't happen."

I thought about that. A lot. And then I realized he was probably right. We can't really disappoint God. He loves us too much. He knows we can't always match up to His perfection. He understands I fall short of His glory. Our weakness and "fallings" are made perfect in Christ. But that doesn't mean I shouldn't try to steady my steps. The day I quit making the effort is the day God cries.

"...for all have sinned and fall short of the glory of God and are justified freely by his grace through the redemption that came by Christ Jesus." Yes, we sin and fall short, but there's no way we can let God down. Not when Christ is lifted up.

When you stumble and fall, remember the place you land is called "grace," so take His hand and stand in "Grace"-land.

Prayer

My God, may I always find peace in Your grace.

BUILDING BLOCKS OF FAITH

Effort means something when you work to improve

He Said, She Said

Journal

....
....
....
....
....
....
....
....
....
....
....
....
....
....
....
....
....
....
....
....
....
....
....
....
....
....
....
....
....
....
....
....

"Hey, Dad, Someone's Calling For You"

He Said

And those he predestined, he also called; those he called, he also justified; those he justified, he also glorified.

Romans 8:30 NIV

Everyone has the power to excel, live with passion and work with purpose. The trick is finding your unique gift.

Years ago, I applied to work for a paper salesman. With an impressive sales record and strong ties within the industry, I assumed they would hire me on the spot. They called two years later, offering me a job.

When I grew tired of selling single-ply, recycled toilet paper, I decided to pursue my love of writing. With a degree in English and Journalism, I figured I'd have little trouble landing a job as a technical writer. Almost a year later IBM called offering me a job as an "html editor." At least "editor" sounded better than "potty paper salesman."

As the web evolved, my work dissolved and soon I was

looking for work again. I remained in my areas of competence, afraid to jump full time into the fickle world of freelance writing, even though I knew I'd been called to write.

Then last spring at a writers conference, a friend asked when I was going to quit my day job and work full time for God.

"I guess that would be now," I said, acknowledging in public the call I felt in my heart.

Paul says those God predestines, He calls. As a people shaped in His image, we're designed for success, wired to work at the thing God calls us to do. There's a popular quotation among Christians that reads; "God doesn't called the equipped. He equips the called." I pray that's true.

A few weeks ago, a ministry called, offering to hire me as their ghost writer. That's when I learned an important lesson about following God's leading. When you start moving to the sound of His voice, He opens doors.

Do you feel bored, burned out and burdened with a nagging sense that you're meant for something more than a dull job in which you're competent but not committed? It just may be that God is calling you to a greater field—His field—a field where you'll be justified, glorified and gratified. If you hear his voice calling, say "yes."

It'll be the best career move you'll ever make.

Prayer

Father, help me to have a grateful heart regardless of my

circumstances.

BUILDING BLOCKS OF FAITH

Never doubt in darkness what God has whispered to you in the

light.

He Said,  Journal

Jump

She Said

*And those he predestined, he also called; those he called, he
also justified; those he justified, he also glorified.*

Romans 8:30 NIV

Cindy K. Hink. That was her name. She kept me company
through a lonely childhood. When there was no one else to
climb trees with or jump rope, Cindy gave me great stories and
adventures through the wooded acre behind our house. When
I was snuggled in the little cave below the giant oak tree, she
eventually showed. Cindy lived in the confines of a very active
imagination and when no one else seemed to care, it was her
who said, "Talk to God."

So I did—squished inside the roots of the old oak tree, I
asked, "God, do ya wanna play?" And Cindy K. Hink whispered,
"He said yes."

As I grew, Cindy K. Hink faded into my memory, but I
never forgot her voice. When I found myself standing alone, peers
shunning me, I could have sworn I heard her say, "He's speaking.
Listen." But I was too busy fighting the demons to hear.

My life swirled out of control at times, and I wondered

why God, who was supposed to love me, ignored me. But the voice reminded me, "Come." I remained faithful and developed a prayer life and when I realized the voice wasn't a childhood fantasy...I ran from it.

I worked a job, kept up the ministry of Christian Devotions, managed my family, worked at church, volunteered, counseled, and wrote until my health began to fail. Yet God kept calling. God, I'm doing what You ask. I'm serving You, I thought.

And He said, "You're doing busy work. Come." My life became so intense I couldn't rest. Health issues grew, tests, trials, until I fell to my knees. Okay. Here I am. What would You have me do?

"Work for me. The earthly pay isn't great but the greater good is something to behold. It won't be easy. You'll sacrifice your comfortable place, but there is greater peace within me. Work for me."

I said yes a few weeks ago. Turned in for my retirement. Opened the door from comfort, stepped into a free-fall and the ground didn't rush up to meet me. Instead, the arms of angels took hold. I've never soared before, not until the other day. And what a rush! Now I know my imaginary childhood friend was really an angel in disguise readying me for God's work—constantly whispering.

God calls us all as Christians into His service. It's not a one-sided relationship. It's not a free ride. It's work, but when He calls, it's up to us to listen. Is God calling you for a task? Listen. Go for the adventure. Say yes and jump!

Prayer

Father, make Yourself known to me. Be present with me.

BUILDING BLOCKS OF FAITH

"Work for the night is coming, when man's work is done."

He Said, *She Said*

Journal

....
....
....
....
....
....
....
....
....
....
....
....
....
....
....
....
....
....
....
....
....
....
....
....
....
....
....
....
....
....
....
....
....
....
....
....

Home Under Construction

Building Permit
He Said

Unless the LORD builds the house,
the builders labor in vain.

Psalm 127:1 NIV

Occasionally our newspaper will list the building permits for development projects. I've noticed that when this happens, sub-contractors and day laborers, not to mention food vendors serving authentic Mexican cuisine, flock to the job site. Lately I've been thinking, "Wouldn't it be great if God announced *His* building plans so we could get in on His next big project?"

Well He does, sort of. There is one building that's always under construction. A Godly home. In our cul-de-sac culture that isolates itself into pods of cookie-cutter neighborhoods, God's basic design for stately architecture remains the same, a home devoted to Him.

The foundation of a Christian home begins with worship. Each day we commit the first fruits of our day to praising Him. In some cases it's little more than, "Thank God it's Saturday, I don't have to go to work." But other days I give thanks for the big blessings like health, shelter and food and the small afflictions like a cold that comes *after* I've finished speaking.

From the praise and worship center, we move down the hall to the library to study His Word. Then it's off to work. Sometimes my wife will wander over to the roll top desk where the bills await. It is here, with trembling fingers, that she offers our tithe to God, for He has challenged us to test Him in this. *"See if I will not open for you the windows of heaven and pour out for you a blessing until it overflows."* So we do and He does.

Later, as we gather around the kitchen table to share our trials and successes, we are reminded to carry each other's burdens. Sometimes after dinner we'll take a walk around the neighborhood because God calls us to love our neighbor as our self and it's hard to do that if you don't even know you *have* neighbors.

Finally, as the day ends and my head hits the pillow, I whisper a final "thank you" for a wife who loves me and for boys who are a joy to love, despite their inability to find the dirty clothes hamper.

Each of us has to find our own way to arrange the rooms, but if you begin with God, love your spouse, serve your family and help your neighbors, you'll construct a fine building that will always appreciate in value—no matter what happens in the housing market.

Prayer

Oh Lord, show me the glory of your temple in this house we call a home.

BUILDING BLOCKS OF FAITH

God honored David's desire to build a holy temple to God.

He'll honor yours, too.

He Said, She Said

Journal

....
....
....
....
....
....
....
....
....
....
....
....
....
....
....
....
....
....
....
....
....
....
....
....
....
....
....
....
....
....

My Home Work Isn't In Vain

She Said

Unless the Lord builds the house, the builders labor in vain.

Psalm 127:1

"Nothing is in vain when you put forth a good effort," she said.

The neighbors probably thought I was insane. My boys would head toward the school bus and I'd be hanging out of the kitchen door shouting, "What are you?"

They'd reply, "Good! Great! Wonderful!"

I'm the eternal optimist. Perhaps it's the result of rearing a disabled son. Positive affirmation was a must for our mentally challenged son's self-esteem and I would do what was necessary to prepare him for life.

From the first time I heard the words, "Your son is, ah... mentally retarded," I knew if Chase was going to thrive, it would be as the result of our own labor.

Call me stubborn—but "I ain't a quitter!" And the more

battles we fought with the school system, the more determined I was to build the necessary foundation Chase would need to be the best he could be.

Many of the life skills we taught him bore no fruit until he reached adulthood, but as a result of years of encouragement, prayers, and trust, my son grew into a fine Christian man.

Some mornings I wondered if shouting positive affirmations at my son would make a difference, but in the end, God blessed my efforts. His heart became a sanctuary for the Father filled with child-like wisdom, a building that will stand for eternity. This was good homework.

Buildings will rise and fall, but a heart built for God will never fail to provide sanctuary for Him and His love.

Do you feel as though your labors are in vain? Invite God into the project. When He oversees the project, the labor is never in vain.

Prayer

Lord, help us build an earthy home from your heavenly plans.

BUILDING BLOCKS OF FAITH

When a stranger knocks on your door, will they find a place of prayer, peace and praise?

Journal

....
....
....
....
....
....
....
....
....
....
....
....
....
....
....
....
....
....
....
....
....
....
....
....
....
....
....
....
....
....
....
....
....
....
....

High Anxiety

He Said

*When anxiety was great within me, your consolation
brought joy to my soul.*

Psalm 94:19 NIV

My plane left an hour late and arrived twenty minutes before my connecting flight. The group of seventeen flying to LA was sure the airline would hold their connection. I knew better. An airline employee in a call center explained she could get me on another flight in the morning. "But you're responsible for your overnight stay," she explained.

I hung up and went looking for a rental. The drive from Atlanta to Raleigh would put me home well after midnight. Then a small voice whispered, "Sit. Take a load off. What's the hurry?"

I sat. Passengers jogged through the terminal, scanned the board for arriving and departing flights, cursed, complained, shouted and cried. I opened my Bible and began to read.

"The Lord is near. Do not be anxious about anything...

the peace of God will guard your hearts." "God is our refuge and strength, an ever-present help in trouble." "The LORD is a refuge for the oppressed, a stronghold in times of trouble." "They will call on me, and I will answer them; I will be with them in trouble, I will deliver them and honor them."

My list of Bible promises was long, but that small voice had told me to rest so I read, relaxed and reviewed my travel options. The longer I watched, the more I saw the people around me the way God sees us—frightened and harried, frantically searching for a way out. But I knew God was aware of my circumstances. He'd known my plane would land late. He was in the moment.

That familiar voice asked, "What do you want?"

To catch a flight to DC, I thought, so I can get home.

"No, what do you really want?"

I thought about it. What I really wanted was to catch a flight to Raleigh. I could get my car from Regan National, later.

My eyes fell upon another verse: "If you, then, though you are evil, know how to give good gifts to your children, how much more will your Father in heaven give good gifts to those who ask him."

So I asked. I wrote a petition in my prayer journal. I thanked God for keeping me safe in my travels. Then I walked to the service desk and asked if there were any available seats on the next flight to Raleigh. A couple of hours later I flew home. The next week, a friend visiting DC drove my van back.

Here's the thing. God isn't a genie. He doesn't grant wishes or deal in whimsical wants. But He does hear our prayers and meet us in our point of need. All that He asks in return is that we trust Him, obey His voice and follow His leading. If we can't trust God for the small things, like a plane ride, how will we ever trust Him with our lives?

Prayer

Lord, help me to trust your timing in every area of my life.

BUILDING BLOCKS OF FAITH

He Said, *She Said*

Journal

....
....
....
....
....
....
....
....
....
....
....
....
....
....
....
....
....
....
....
....
....
....
....
....
....
....
....
....
....
....
....
....
....

Pray for your needs and watch expectantly for God's answer.

Keep Back a Dollar

She Said

*When anxiety was great within me, your consolation
brought joy to my soul.*

Psalm 94:19 NIV

"Eight dollars! That's it?" I asked the teller. "But there was plenty of money in the account this morning. What happened? I've not spent it!"

The teller shrugged. "What would you like me to do?"

My stomach turned and my face grew warm. I wasn't sure what to do. I only knew the feelings of terror and panic that crept into my mind. This was a place God knew I hated. I'd spent seven years under the darkness of loneliness and fear when I had nothing—scrapped to feed my boys. This spot, the place where survival kicked in, was a territory I didn't want to visit again... ever! Memories flooded back. Days when eight dollars was the equivalent of $8,000.00. I pleaded that God would pull me out of poverty and place me into peace.

Fear squeezed the joy from me and replaced it with guilt

and unworthiness. Until today, God had not let the ministry account dip into single digits. He knew my fear. So why today? Why test me today?

My anxiety dragged me to a place of faithlessness. The love and joy I'd found in this ministry suddenly dissipated. I was hurt, angry and a little disappointed that God would put me in this situation again, especially since this was HIS ministry. We were just the tools.

I stared at the last $300 in our savings account then instructed the teller to move it to checking. Walking out of the bank, I leaned against the wall and cried. With over $2000 in bills hovering over the ministry, the meager $300 would be gone end-of-day.

God tests us, tries us and even pushes occasionally to stretch beyond our immediate knowledge of Him. He invites us through hardships to explore His peace that passes understanding and to claim His promises of consolation, joy and the plan He has to bless us, not harm us. It's not easy and He brought me to my knees kicking and screaming.

"Just trust me," He whispered.

I crawled in the car and headed to the post office. Slipping my key into the box, I looked up and cried, "God provide." Twisting the key, I opened the door, and an envelope lay tilted to one side. A smile parted my lips and when I opened the letter, a sigh of relief came over me.

God promises when our anxiety is the greatest, trust it to Him, we'll receive consolation and joy. That day, I learned it wasn't about me, but whether I had a willing heart to learn, to stretch, to see a new side of Christ, and when I said yes, the elation of peace was immeasurable.

When anxiety overwhelms your heart, seek the promises of His consolation and joy. There is peace in handing over the worry.

The envelope...contained a check for $300. God matched what we had and we paid the first bill.

Prayer

Lord, provide.

BUILDING BLOCKS OF FAITH

He Said, *She Said*

Journal

....
....
....
....
....
....
....
....
....
....
....
....
....
....
....
....
....
....
....
....
....
....
....
....
....
....
....
....
....
....
....

"You have to believe. Just believe." – Peter Pan

We're Broke

He Said

...God loves a cheerful giver. And God is able to bless you abundantly, so that in all things at all times, having all that you need, you will abound in every good work.

2 Corinthians 9: 7-8 NIV

Financial disagreements are a normal and necessary part of any marriage, especially when you're broke. In any discussion between two people who are, financially speaking, eating from the same dog dish, there will always been a certain amount of tension. Tension that, over time, leads to even more disagreements over such petty purchases as milk, bread and motorcycles.

That's why, when it comes to financial matters, you should make every effort to show compassion, a willingness to compromise, and, if you have one, a prenuptial agreement protecting your assets. Whenever my wife calls a budget meeting, I know it's a serious matter. That's why I pause the game, fix a snack and hide in the garage. Sometimes this strategy works, but when it doesn't I take refuge in God's law of the harvest, which says he who sows sparingly reaps sparingly so spend all you can when you can before she can.

If you're like most couples in financial trouble, you're desperate for practical advice, so here are five steps you can take that will lead to, if not financial independence, at least more arguments.

First, get rid of credit card debt. According to the latest figures, the average American household owes nearly $9,200 in credit card debt. One way to reduce your debt is to ask Congress to assume your bad loans. Sure, they could say "no" but even if they do, you can change their mind with a generous campaign contribution charged, of course, to your credit card. Second, not all debt is bad. Spending money on golf clubs, chrome rims or a vacation in the Bahamas is okay. Borrowing for a home or college is not.

Third, make a list of long-term financial goals. Then ignore them. No point stressing over something that's not going to happen, but at least you can *say* you're planning for the future. Fourth, go shopping with your wife. Every year women spend thousands of dollars on shoes, hair coloring treatments and those little cotton balls that fill up the waste basket. Obviously, women need help in the buying department. If men understand anything, it's how to shop wisely. Just look at our huge collection of screwdrivers, socket sets and adjustable wrenches.

Finally, remember that God loves a cheerful giver, so the

next time your buddy needs help paying his green fees offer to split the cost of the golf cart.

God has promised to bless abundantly. We only need ask, sow generously and trust Him. That is, after all, what it says on the legal tender I once called "my allowance." Abound in good work and if you can't do that, then just work.

Prayer

Lord, I know everything is Yours and You give abundantly but could You give me an advance on next month's blessing?

BUILDING BLOCKS OF FAITH

It's not a matter of how much you possess but how much your possessions matter to you.

He Said, *She Said*

Journal

We're Blessed

She Said

...God loves a cheerful giver. And God is able to bless you abundantly, so that in all things at all times, having all that you need, you will abound in every good work.

2 Corinthians 9: 7-8 NIV

$142,048.00! I couldn't believe the bill was so large but our insurance company was refusing to pay our son's medical expenses. I panicked, emptied our saving and spread the rest of the costs among credit cards. Stupid? Perhaps. But a mother will do almost anything for her child. I'm not sure what my husband would have done. I didn't ask. I just knew there was price to pay for giving birth to a boy with a handicap and no matter what the cost, I wouldn't deny Chase the care he needed.

I had a slush fund with $50 set aside. Mad money for me. It wasn't much, but it was *mine*. With our savings gone, credit cards maxed out and creditors calling daily, we began to fall behind on the monthly interest payments. And still I wouldn't touch my secret stash or ask God for help. I'd manage on my own, thank you.

Then one evening, in the garden, I broke down. "God, help us," I cried. "I can't do this anymore." That's when it began to rain. Not money. But cold, hard drops. I thought it was some kind of sick joke, God's way of punishing me for...well, I wasn't sure for what. I'd done the best I knew how. But there I was broke, wet and on my knees in the mud. That's when I accused God of acting like a heartless bill collector.

The next day I cleaned out my slush fund. Not to pay the bills, but to help a starving college student buy food. I figured I could help someone else even if God refused to help me. I could be bigger and more charitable than God, even if I was bitter.

The next week I opened the mail and found a check for $100. Within days more money arrived from mysterious sources. Since that day on my knees in the mud, God has provided thousands of dollars in ways I'd never imagined. I learned that when I give, He gives more.

I don't look at the balance in my slush fund anymore. I just give with a joyful heart. As I write this I know that my secret stash is empty. I cleaned it out last week to help a ministry that's dear to my heart. But I'm not worried. God will provide. He always has. He always will. I only needed to let go, trust and fall to my knees in prayer.

Prayer

Lord, teach me to open my fist and give freely.

BUILDING BLOCKS OF FAITH

Give as Jesus gave. Set aside $50 and then give when someone in need asks, give. God is investing in you. Grow with interest.

He Said, *She Said*

Journal

....
....
....
....
....
....
....
....
....
....
....
....
....
....
....
....
....
....
....
....
....
....
....
....
....
....
....
....
....
....
....
....
....
....
....
....
....
....
....
....

Making a Dollar Go A Long Way

He Said

Give generously to them [the poor] and do so without a grudging heart; then because of this the LORD your God will bless you in all your work and in everything you put your hand to.

Deuteronomy 15:10 NIV

A few weeks ago, I found a dollar lying on the sidewalk. Occasionally during my walks, I'll find a penny or nickel or a nickel-plated hubcap, but seldom cash. I stuffed the bill in my pocket and continued on, thinking as I walked, how I'd spend the money. Of course, first I'd tithe this unexpected blessing; give the dime to some charity. But that would leave me a few cents short of a ninety-nine cents menu item at our local fast food restaurant. Maybe I could just owe God the ten cents, I thought. Pay Him back on Sunday.

Then I decided the free dollar was a pop quiz, God's way of testing me to see if I could be trusted with a small amount.

I got excited. Pass this and it could be that he'll give me lots of dollars. But I also knew you couldn't buy God's favor with false motives. Still, it was just a dollar. And it wasn't like I had to have it to eat.

We came to an intersection. The dog began barking at a paper bag rolling across the grass the way she does every time trash, cats and squirrels refuse to cower at her threats. The light changed. We walked on.

The middle-class men of Israel walked on, too. Hoarding their wealth, cheating their neighbor. Acting with contempt toward the foreigners living on their land. So God warned them, "...do not be hardhearted or tightfisted toward your poor brother...There should be no poor among you, for in the land the LORD your God is giving you to possess as your inheritance, he will richly bless you."

Just like He's blessed us, I thought.

Centuries later He sent His Son, warning them again. "I tell you the truth, whatever you did not do for one of the least of these, you did not do for me."

The least of these...The poor, the immigrant, the ignorant, the illegal.

These were my thoughts as I walked through my upper-middle class neighborhood clutching my dollar. I looked upon the large homes with manicured lawns and I recalled how, after we'd moved into the neighborhood, the taco truck would park across the street. There, construction crews gathered, eating and laughing and listening to the sounds of mariachi bands on the radio. Now those sounds were gone. So, too, were the men.

A block from my house I passed a brother and sister selling lemonade. They'd erected their stand at the base of a sidewalk leading to the apartment complex where the gangs live. Their skin had the coco tint of the Aztec, the large brown eyes and hesitant smile of the fearful.

"Limonada?"

"No, but here's a dollar, anyway," I said. "It's the least I can do."

The least I can do...The least of these...

When we give graciously, a dollar can go a long way. It can change a child, change a future, change a culture. Perhaps, it can even go so far as to change our hearts.

Prayer

Father, help me to trust you no matter how much
or little I have.

BUILDING BLOCKS OF FAITH

Worshiping wealth is merely serving a smaller god.

He Said, *She Said*

Journal

....
....
....
....
....
....
....
....
....
....
....
....
....
....
....
....
....
....
....
....
....
....
....
....
....
....
....
....
....
....
....
....
....
....
....

A Little Goes a Long Way!

She Said

Give generously to them and do so without a grudging heart; then because of this the LORD your God will bless you in all your work and in everything you put your hand to.

Deuteronomy 15:10 NIV

She looked pale, her eyes sunken but her smile was unfailing. The perky college sophomore bounced into the church sanctuary, waving toward us. She was a petite girl, but that day, she looked especially thin.

"How are you sweetie?"

"Great! Can't complain." She wrapped her bony arms around my neck and hugged.

"You feel way too skinny, girl. Aren't you eating?"

Her smile faded. "I can't lie. I'm strapped. With my brother being sick, mom losing her job and me being in college, I've been

218

trying to take up the slack. Been eating crackers, mostly."

The 20-year-old, full-time college student cared for two families on her full-time, minimum wage salary. The child was starving. She'd sacrificed her own needs to give to her family.

We weren't in a great financial spot ourselves. Our own son's medical needs had left us literally saving pennies in a jar. But the day before, we'd taken $100 from the jar to buy our groceries, with our spare change for our empty cupboards.

Slipping my hand into my purse I pulled out the $100 bill and pressed it into her palm. "Take this and buy groceries."

A tear dripped off her cheek.

Giving is hard at times. Especially when our needs appear to outweigh the needs of others. But how do we know, really? All we know for certain is that God instructs us to give to the poor, to those in need, without hesitation, without strings, but with a generous heart.

Two years later, I saw that girl again. Newly married, she and her husband now held good jobs. She wasn't wealthy, but she wasn't starving, either. Pulling out her checkbook she scribbled a check for $400.

"Here," she said, handing me the check. "This is your money back, plus interest."

"Not my money. God's. And it wasn't a loan. It was a gift. I can't take it."

Her faced dropped. "Then what can I do for you?"

"It's enough to know you're happy and successful. Now, if you really want to do something for us, give that money to four students who, now, are like you were, then."

A week later she sent a list of students she'd helped. Later we found our friend had requested the same thing of the students she'd given money to. They gave to others, as well. Long before the movie, God had already introduced the concept of Pay It Forward. All we did was obey and honor His word. Now, fifteen years later, the Starving Student Award continues to be awarded to a select group of students at East Tennessee State University.

God blesses those who give wholeheartedly. Do you see a need that should be met? Make a difference and give generously. A little given without hesitation goes a long way.

Prayer

My Lord, lead us in our giving. May our gifts glorify Your name.

BUILDING BLOCKS OF FAITH

Take time to give to a student in need. Your gift may change a

He Said, She Said

Journal

....
....
....
....
....
....
....
....
....
....
....
....
....
....
....
....
....
....
....
....
....
....
....
....
....
....
....
....
....
....
....
....
....
....
....

life.

Church of the Doubting Saint Thomas

He Said

And let us consider how we may spur one another on toward love and good deeds, not giving up meeting together, as some are in the habit of doing, but encouraging one another—and all the more as you see the Day approaching.

Hebrews 10:24-25 NIV

My bride and I went church hunting the other day. If you've ever tried to find a church then you know how difficult this can be, since most churches meet at the same time—on weekends and too early—which is why I decided to start my own church. I'm calling it Saint Thomas. Wait, there's already a St. Thomas, but it costs a lot to fly there. Plus, on Tuesdays, when the cruise ships are in port, the business district gets really crowded and smells like Desenex. Okay, so my new church will be the Church of the Doubting Saint Thomas.

My church will only have one rule—doubt everything, trust

no one, and in church softball when a fly ball is hit to the outfield the runner must tag up before leaving the bag. Okay, that's three rules, so we'll have to change the charter. Our mission statement will be "Oh yeah, prove it." If our pastor wants to do something dumb, like add an extra service to accommodate more members, we'll say "No way. You don't even visit the sick folks we have." Should the Board of Trustees attempt to spend money on landscaping we'll say "Not with our dollars you won't. God got by with weeds and crab grass, we can, too." If the choir director wants to lead us in some new songs, we'll say "How Great Thou Art going to look standing in the unemployment line." And don't even think about adding a contemporary service with drums, guitars and videos. We're talking church, here, not a Bon Jovi concert.

I asked my bride what she wanted in a new church. She said lots of parking places, breath mints on the pews and sermons that lasted no longer than ten minutes—she was adamant on this point. Children in diapers would be prohibited from attending adult worship services and communion would be by invitation only to make sure sick people didn't contaminate the cups and wafers. As you can see creating, the perfect church is going to be hard.

In fact, we were so tired from thinking about it that we decided to sleep in Sunday, but then, as I was getting my paper from the mailbox, our neighbor walked over and invited us to a fellowship brunch. I hated to say no because, honestly, my wife's not much of a cook on Sundays.

I went and found the parking lot packed, the shuttle too slow and the praise band practicing in the room next to our Sunday School class. I was ready to bolt, but my wife got roped into a women's study on the Book of Ruth. Now I'm stuck, but as soon as she's finished, I'm outta here. Only...there's a golf outing coming up and my wife really wants to sing in the Christmas Cantata. Okay, we'll stay through Christmas. Or maybe January, because they've got that "Souper Bowl Party" thing going on. February, we're definitely gone then. Church, who'd have thought finding a church home could be so hard... and so much fun.

Prayer

Lord, help me catch your vision for our church, get plugged in and give back.

BUILDING BLOCKS OF FAITH

God has entrusted his church to people. Like, love and serve

He Said, *She Said*

Journal

....
....
....
....
....
....
....
....
....
....
....
....
....
....
....
....
....
....
....
....
....
....
....
....
....
....
....
....
....
....
....

others.

Church, It's Habit Forming

She Said

*And let us consider how we may spur one another on
toward love and good deeds, not giving up meeting together,
as some are in the habit of doing, but encouraging one
another—and all the more as you see the Day approaching.*

Hebrews 10:24-25 NIV

They say that you can establish a habit in thirty days.
Repeat an action often enough and you'll be hooked. My mother
established the habit of going to church when I was a toddler. We
rarely missed a service. I'm still stuck on church, only now it's a
habit of genuine love for my Father.

I've have tried to raise my boys to know Christ and to be
a part of His church, but it's hard pulling teens from a bed on
weekends—especially when your spouse isn't supportive and
unwilling to lead by example. Kids, boys especially, pick up on
the clues of their dad.

I have friends who give their children the *option* of attending church. The kids complain about the early hour and whine about getting dressed until mom says, "It's okay, you don't have to go if you don't want to." Want to go? What child has ever wanted to do anything but sulk, sass and sleep on the weekends? They're teenagers, not an intelligent life form.

I've been tempted to stay home on Sundays. In fact, I lived with a husband who turned his back on the church and refused to go. I know from experience what it's like to drag my kids out on a cold winter morning, stuff them in car seats and race to church alone. But that's what you do if you want to set a habit for life. Sure, they *might* find Christ outside the church. Others have. But do you really want to risk your child's eternal future to a chance encounter at the mall?

To a large degree, how we encourage our children determines the steps they will take and the direction they will go. Have I always been successful? No. My boys have disappointed me and broken my heart. Right now there's one I can't find at all. But I did what I could. I did my best.

A minister once told me not to worry about the eternal life of my mentally retarded son. He said Chase was covered by the mercy of Christ. "But," he said, raising his finger, "You have the responsibility to establish the habit, to teach him that God is important." My job is to get him to church. God's work is to save him.

Have you been tempted to roll over, sleep in and stray from the church? Don't do it. Be the example. Teach what it means to be a family grounded in Christ. Then give your children room to find their own church family in the body of Christ for that too, is His will.

Prayer

My God, help me to be the example, set the habit and be the body of *your* church.

BUILDING BLOCKS OF FAITH

The hardest part of church is showing up.